Praise for *Queer*

"Incredibly clear, beautifully written explanat[...]
and its inherent queerness, written with style [...] an expert in the
subject."

— Yvonne Aburrow, author of *All Acts of Love & Pleasure: Inclusive Wicca*

"Sensitive and deeply intentional, *Queer Qabala* revels in the glory of the
gorgeous strangeness inherent in existing outside the typical box. Enfys J.
Book is a warm and kind guide through a complex system, providing an
exceptional and deeply needed resource for modern Pagan practitioners."

— Courtney Weber, author of *Hekate* and *The Morrigan*

"Book's exploration of the queerness inherent in this Hermetic descendant
of Jewish mystical tradition is nothing short of revelatory."

— Misha Magdalene, author of *Outside the Charmed Circle*

"Enfys carefully removes layers of misconceptions to reveal the truth that
the Qabala contains everyone and everything, including all that is yet to
be discovered or defined. This book is not just for queer people, it is for
everyone. If you are a seeker of the mysteries and on the path of spiritual
evolution, the material in this book is indispensable because it opens new
realms of thought."

— Ivo Dominguez Jr., author of *The Four Elements of the Wise*

"Whether you're new to the Tree of Life concept or have been exploring
the Sephirot for years, Enfys J. Book's fresh perspectives unveil the magical potential the Qabala holds for the queer practitioner."

— Mat Auryn, bestselling author of *Psychic Witch*

"Enfys skillfully challenges long-standing assumptions and redefines an
ancient system to bring it in line with the realities of the modern world.
Their revisioning of the spheres and paths of the Hermetic Qabala to
reveal its inherent inclusivity and remove limiting gender assignments is
a much-needed change … If you've avoided learning or working with the
Qabala because you didn't feel like you fit within its patriarchal limits,
read this book."

— Diotima Mantineia, astrologer and author
of *Touch the Earth, Kiss the Sky*

"Enfys J. Book brings all the vitality and joy of queer culture to this book, combining serious magical reflection with a vibrant celebration of the diversity in human gender, sex, and sexuality. *Queer Qabala* shows us not only that Qabala can be welcoming to queer magical practitioners, but that it already is."

—Jack Chanek, author of *Qabalah for Wiccans*

"*Queer Qabala* provides a fresh perspective to the understanding of Hermetic Qabala. It is an invitation to all magickal practitioners to explore, redefine, and ultimately claim the studies of Qabala as a system that is universal in its application and inclusive in its use."

—Robin Fennelly, author of *Poetry of the Spheres*

"Thank you, Enfys J. Book, for being the one to guide us through the mists of binary vision that cloud so much of our current worldview … As Enfys reminds us: this is a system that seeks to describe the universe, so let's allow it to reflect the diversity of those who approach it and recognize its true depth and breadth."

—Jane Meredith, author of *Falling Through the Tree of Life*

"What is so revolutionary about this book is that it doesn't project a queer sensibility onto an existing, oppressive paradigm, but instead explores the inherent (and traditional!) queerness of the Qabala, offering a lens that is at once both traditional as well as relevant to an evolving consciousness. Besides being an extremely important book for the queer occultist, this is also a sound introduction to the Qabala in general, offering practitioners a greater understanding of the Tree of Life and how to work with it toward the betterment of their lives."

—Storm Faerywolf, author of *The Satyr's Kiss*

QUEER
QABALA

About the Author

Enfys J. Book (they/them) is the creative force behind Major Arqueerna, a website dedicated to queerness and magickal practice, particularly the Qabala. They are clergy (third degree) of the Assembly of the Sacred Wheel, a syncretic Wiccan tradition based in the mid-Atlantic. They were the first openly nonbinary clergy member initiated within the tradition and serve as high priest of the Fellowship of the Ancient White Stag coven in the Washington, D.C. metro area. They have been working closely with Qabala since 2012, teaching classes on magickal practice since 2015, and teaching classes on Qabala and Queer Magick since 2017. As a bisexual, nonbinary Pagan, they employ a queer lens to break down limiting binaries in magickal theory and practice, and advocate for bisexual, transgender, nonbinary/genderqueer, queer, and asexual visibility and inclusion.

Enfys is a founding member of the Misbehavin' Maidens, a band that describes their music as "funny, filthy, feminist, fandom folk." The band seeks to promote sex-positive and queer-inclusive feminism through music.

Enfys lives in Maryland and has worked as a web content strategist and project manager since 2001.

They can be reached in many places on the internet:

majorarqueerna.com

twitter.com/majorarqueerna

facebook.com/majorarqueerna

instagram.com/majorarqueerna

info@majorarqueerna.com

QUEER
QABALA

Nonbinary, Genderfluid, Omnisexual Mysticism & Magick

ENFYS J. BOOK

FOREWORD BY **CHRISTOPHER PENCZAK**

Llewellyn Publications • Woodbury, Minnesota

FIRST EDITION
Second Printing, 2022

Book design by Valerie A. King
Cover design by Shira Atakpu
Figure on page 210 © Mary Ann Zapalac
Interior illustrations by Llewellyn Art Department

Llewellyn Publications is a registered trademark of Llewellyn Worldwide Ltd.

Library of Congress Cataloging-in-Publication Data
Names: Book, Enfys J., author.
Title: Queer qabala : nonbinary, genderfluid, omnisexual mysticism & magick
  / Enfys J. Book.
Other titles: Queer cabala
Description: First edition. | Woodbury, Minnesota : Llewellyn Publications,
  a division of Llewellyn Worldwide Ltd, 2022. | Includes bibliographical
  references. | Summary: "Enfys J. Book explains the basics of Qabala in
  an easy-to-understand way and highlights the inherent queer and
  nonbinary nature of this powerful mystical system as well as the innate
  inclusivity of its practice. This book offers a variety of pathworkings,
  exercises, and spells to deepen understanding"—Provided by publisher.
Identifiers: LCCN 2022006473 (print) | LCCN 2022006474 (ebook) | ISBN
  9780738769769 (paperback) | ISBN 9780738769967 (ebook)
Subjects: LCSH: Cabala. | Sexual minorities. | Magic. | Sefirot (Cabala) |
  Cabala—Problems, exercises, etc.
Classification: LCC BF1623.C2 B67 2022 (print) | LCC BF1623.C2 (ebook) |
  DDC 135/.47—dc23/eng/20220321
LC record available at https://lccn.loc.gov/2022006473
LC ebook record available at https://lccn.loc.gov/2022006474

Llewellyn Publications
A Division of Llewellyn Worldwide Ltd.
2143 Wooddale Drive
Woodbury, MN 55125-2989
www.llewellyn.com

Printed in the United States of America

Dedication

To my mentors.

CONTENTS

EXERCISES

ACKNOWLEDGMENTS

The idea of queer Qabala abruptly and somewhat rudely knocked on my brain just after I'd finished creating and leading a year-long series of Qabala classes and rituals for my coven in 2017. I don't remember the exact moment, but I remember ringing up one of my teachers, Ivo Dominguez Jr., saying, "I see a ton of queer stuff here—am I off base?" And he said no, I wasn't. Encouraged by this, I continued to pull on that thread, and the more I did, the deeper I fell down this rabbit hole of "Wow, Qabala is actually *super* queer." And now you have a book in your hands: the result of my obsession.

So I have Ivo to thank, not only for guiding me in my early Qabala studies and proctoring my work on Qabala, but also for encouraging me to continue this line of academic inquiry and write this book. Thank you, Ivo.

My friend Irene Glasse helped me stay accountable in working toward the goal of a finished book. For the much-needed structure, well-timed enthusiasm, and symbiotic partnership, thank you, Irene.

My partner, Niall Sheehan, supported me, encouraged me, and never doubted me once throughout this wacky process. Thank you, my love.

Misha Magdalene's *Outside the Charmed Circle* was a huge influence on the thought process that brought me to write *Queer Qabala,* and I'm lucky enough to call Misha a friend as well. Many thanks, Misha: you gave me the courage to believe in myself and my message.

Ivo, Irene, and Misha were also beta readers of this book, along with Jeff Bleam. All of them helped make this book better, and I deeply appreciate their time and constructive feedback.

I learned so many things that informed this book from so many people, particularly those in my spiritual tradition, the Assembly of the Sacred Wheel. In addition to those named above, I particularly give thanks to Robin Fennelly, Michael Smith, Jon Beschen, Jim Welch, Mark Pemburn, Leanne Pemburn, Jim Dickinson, Monica Stanton, and Gwendolyn Reece.

To those whose written works helped crystalize my thoughts around queerness and magick, I give thanks: Meg-John Barker, Jules Scheele, Alex Iantaffi, Cassandra Snow, Lee Harrington, Rachel Pollack, and T. Thorn Coyle.

To those who have encouraged my writing along the way, I give thanks: My parents, Jane and Dick Larsen; Stephen Blackmoore; Chuck Wendig; Kevin Hearne; Courtney Weber; Barbara Campbell; Dr. Jessica Hebert; Sunnie Larsen; Alyssa Yeager; Anton Teach Blackthorn; Dr. Phoebe Hamilton; and Marnie Twigg.

Finally, many thanks to Llewellyn and my editor, Heather Greene, for taking a chance on this newbie author, and for helping to make this book the best it could be. Thanks, also, to Christopher Penczak for lending his time and talents to writing the foreword for this, my very first published book. I am honored and humbled.

FOREWORD

What I remember best about my first studies in Hermetic Qabala and ceremonial magick was getting a few shocks along the way. A common practice is to start at the bottom of the figure known as the Tree of Life and learn meditations, rituals, and teachings as one rises through the Tree, with concepts becoming more esoteric and ephemeral the higher you go until you reach the Qabalistic concept of the godhead.

Each point along the Tree has a range of correspondences, colors, scents, images, astrology, and archetypes. The images of Hermetic Qabala are often drawing upon ancient Pagan myths and deities, and as in the nature of the Qabala, alternate between images of goddesses and gods, though with often surprising twists, and these twists show up in ways different than you might expect. The first twist was in the teaching that what is commonly aligned with feminine and masculine archetypes or energy—concepts of receptivity and projectivity—reverse when you cross the first threshold, the veil separating the bottom of the Tree from the middle. The feminine becomes the active aspect on the inner planes and the masculine the receptive.

This made some folks in the study group rather upset, because it went against what they considered to be a truth regarding the feminine and masculine forces in magick and in life. While all of the members of this group accepted me as a gay man, they still had their strong assumptions about occultism and polarity, about gender and the "fertility" of magick.

And Qabala caused them to question their assumptions, when they assumed that it would simply affirm what they already knew to be true. While I was surprised too, I found their difficulties with the ideas even more surprising, but it left me feeling a bit more empowered than before, as if I had the weight of ancient authority on "my" side.

As I teach Hermetic Qabala now, particularly to Witches, I go through the same process with at least one student every time, if not an entire group of students. It provides one of the first key mysteries of the Qabala: What is true on one level is false on another. What is false at one level can be true on another. Things are not locked into one shape, one form, or one way of being. Expectations must shift as consciousness shifts, and new expressions are found.

I can't think of anything queerer than a system describing reality that will always push you to get out of your assumptions of how it should be simply because that was what was true at a previous stage. The secret of the evolution of the teachings is embedded right within them, a lesson I've seen time and again. Qabala is a living practice and grows with each generation that studies it as they contribute symbols and concepts to the growing body of wisdom. The lower spheres challenge us with images of the Moon's realm embodied by a slumbering and erect young man—not what most Pagans imagine when they come to the Moon. The sphere of Mercury was embodied by the alchemical hermaphrodite imagery, not just the wing-footed, decidedly male, messenger god. The masculine warrior sphere of Mars could be a goddess of war. Expectations kept getting twisted when I first studied, and I love seeing that happen as I teach. It leaves me open to all the new interpretations to come.

The second twist was at the threshold between the middle and the top of the Tree, divided not by a veil, but by the abyss. There you could find, or maybe not find, the invisible point on the Tree known as Da'ath, meaning knowledge. This was the gateway to the Tree of Evil, the Tree of Death, the Nightside of Eden, and the reverse of all things good. At least that is what people said. Some magicians get obsessed with it, and I can see why. Looking at the world, it is easy to get discouraged or become obsessed with the destruction, violence, and harm of the world—the evil. It seems to be everywhere.

As a queer Witch, I saw and felt that evil a lot growing up in a time that was far less open than today, and while I'd like to say the evils of the world have diminished, many have simply grown and changed form. Yet again, the secret was embedded in the teachings. The "opposite" of the emanation of the Tree of Life, the qlippoth, translated to "shell" or "husk," showing that the reverse Tree was not one of active and oppositional evil, a monster lurking in the night, but the absence of divinity. The seed of the concept, the core of it, was gone, leaving just the husk. The shell of power is the absence of divine power. The shell of love is the absence of divine love. The Nightside of Eden is simply a broken structure, and it's often in brokenness that evil is done, though it's not inherent or divine evil. It's simply an absence, a loss. The whole concept of the reverse Tree helped me reframe the evil I saw in the world and encountered in my own life, and encouraged the potential for healing: the understanding that Da'ath was the gateway and Da'ath means knowledge—that the obsession with knowledge lacking wisdom was the way to be trapped in this world of shells. Just because you can do something doesn't mean you should. Living in an age of information shows us how knowledge alone can cause us to sink into our own abyss.

The last twist, the shock for many, was in the godhead, the symbol of the divine beyond all symbols. For some it was an empty throne, but often it was the icon of the bearded man in profile, the typical patriarch of the Old Testament. But was it? The bearded man was also a symbol of the second point on the Tree: Wisdom, also known as Chokmah. For Kether, it was specifically a bearded man in profile. What Qabala teachers often teach is if the figure turns from profile, you'll see one who is half bearded male, half heavenly queen. Together, they expressed a form of what used to be called the subversive "genderfuck" image of the queer community, a mode of self-expression that continues to unfold in many ways, often mixing gender expressions in both artistic and confrontational styles. One of my favorites is the bearded "nuns" of the Sisters of

Perpetual Indulgence. Essentially on some level, in my magickal worldview, the godhead became a genderfuck drag queen/king, a multitude of expressions of the sacred androgyne. It wasn't a subtle blend of gender qualities into something safe and heavenly, but a subversive, in-your-face expression of all the traits at once. And Qabala teachers tell us to keep in mind, the godhead only "looked" human to us in visionary magick because we were human. That form could work with us, but in truth, it wasn't just all genders, but all things at the same time. Again, I thought you couldn't get queerer than that.

Hermetic Qabala lulls you in with its seeming standard roles and images, its gender associations and polarities of energy, a system of traditional symbolism that can get the modern seeker upset at first, as it appears to be locked in a past age. What it is really doing is preparing your consciousness for these mysteries that will defy your expectations if you pursue them wholeheartedly and openheartedly. Hermetic Qabala is subversive. Each generation will add to the growing, evolving understanding of the tradition, presenting the timeless wisdoms in the context of their own time, place, and culture.

And this is what Enfys J. Book is doing in this text: not asking, "Is Qabala queer?" at the various stages and lessons, but instead asking, "What makes Qabala queer?" Like the alchemists of old, they reveal what is inner to the outer, showing clearly what has always been there. Throughout the chapters, Enfys brings the queer reader through the life journey of our shared common experiences and how they apply to the Tree of Life, and for the non-queer reader, shows how their life might be queerer than they think, for these experiences can be a part of all our lives in some form. Adding to the symbol system of the modern lexicon, they bring figures such as the superhero Squirrel Girl to the realm of Geburah and show how might is being expressed today. Spider-Man, old and new, Peter Parker and Miles Morales, become the symbol of the "leaper between," jumping across the abyss. If you are unfamiliar with these superheroes, have no fear, for the work is experiential, taking the reader up the Tree in meditation, and down the Tree through practical ritual. You'll find your own superheroes and icons around the way and become comfortable with those that don't necessarily fit what you might believe is the Qabalistic mold of traditional occultism. Everything is a part of the Tree of Life.

If you are new to the Qabala, this is certainly going to open the door for you. If you are well versed in the tradition, it might challenge your past experiences, but what could be more Qabalistic than that?

—Christopher Penczak
Samhain 2021

INTRODUCTION

I fell in love with Qabala despite myself.

Nothing about me screams, *This person should absolutely study Hermetic Qabala*. Like many people who were raised Christian and veered into Paganism as adults, I flinch when I see biblical imagery in my magickal texts. Like many queer people, I also have a strong distaste for anything that appears to lean heavily on patriarchal symbolism and binary gender metaphors. And as an intelligent kid who grew into an impatient adult, I also tend to balk at things I can't instantly understand and begin using.

And yet, here I am: a queer, Pagan, Hermetic Qabala nerd.

What is Qabala, and why do I love it so much? Qabala is a framework for understanding ourselves and the universe using a glyph called the Tree of Life. I began studying Qabala because I wanted to know what made magick work. I wanted to understand the underpinnings of modern magickal systems, castings, and rituals—particularly those of my tradition, the Assembly of the Sacred Wheel, which uses Qabala extensively. I needed to know how people developed spells and how they could hold a lot of different, complex magickal systems in their heads simultaneously, like tarot and astrology. As I dug deeper into Qabala, though, I became as much fascinated as I was frustrated by its complexity. Spheres and paths, variations on the glyph over time, multiple Trees in multiple worlds, not to mention endless lists and tables of correspondences… there was just so much *there* that I could chew on and ponder. Though I desired to instantly understand it, I ultimately came to appreciate that you could study Qabala for a lifetime and only begin to scratch the surface of understanding it. Qabala's complexity is part of its beauty.

A dear, departed friend of mine, Vickie Edrington, used to say that magick adds poetry to science. For me, Qabala is a type of science to accompany and describe that poetry: a sort of unified theory of magick.

And, dear reader, Qabala is *so very* queer. It's an incredibly affirming magickal tool for queer people, and I'm excited to show you all the ways in which it is.

Notice that I said Qabala *is* queer and not *could be considered to be* queer. That word choice is intentional. This book is not about arbitrarily, tenuously aligning queer concepts to Qabala as a gimmick. I am not reinventing Qabala, because it doesn't need to be reinvented. The fundamentals of what makes Qabala queer have been part of Qabala for centuries. However, it is incumbent upon every generation of Qabalists to add to the depth of knowledge and understanding of the Tree. This book is my attempt at doing so by pointing out ways in which Qabala is a queer spiritual tool and uncovering ways in which queer people may find it useful in their spiritual practice by relating it to their lived experience.

Beyond Inclusion

In part, this book was written out of frustration, because books on Qabala tend to range from "attempting to be inclusive but still really wedded to binary gender concepts" to "deeply problematic." The older the book, the worse the problematic content. From Gareth Knight's homophobic asides in *A Practical Guide to Qabalistic Symbolism* to Dion Fortune's casual racism in *The Mystical Qabalah*, the Qabala texts of the first half of the twentieth century were written by people who had no problem expressing racist, sexist, homophobic, and ableist ideas in their books. Unfortunately, these books are often touted as starter texts, and the authors' not-remotely-hidden biases can turn off a lot of would-be Qabalists.

Indeed, some magickal practitioners quickly dismiss Qabala as antiquated, hierarchical, patriarchal, or just plain useless in a modern magickal context. If you examine only the surface, you may see a magickal system representative of Abrahamic religions' understanding of the relationship between ultimate divinity and humanity: divinity is way up there in heaven—represented by a bearded man, no less—and humanity is way down here at the bottom, with lots of stuff between us and divinity. You may roll your eyes at references to *masculine* and *feminine* pillars aligned with the concepts of *mercy* and *severity*. You may quirk an eyebrow at the moral judgments inherent in assigning each sphere a *virtue* and a *vice*. It's easy to see how modern occultists might be turned off Qabala at first glance.

However, in the words of queer Pagan author Misha Magdalene:

> *It's easy to look at the misguided parts of a tradition*
> *or the hypocrisy of its leaders and conclude that there's*
> *nothing of value to be found in the tradition itself.*
> *It's much harder, but can also be more rewarding,*
> *to discern what there is in a tradition that's good*
> *and worthwhile, independent of the logical or moral*
> *failings of the human beings within it.*[1]

Qabala is an incredibly rich and dense magickal symbol and tool, and scholars have had to work hard to make it relatable, often employing metaphors to do so. For example, the metaphor of *masculine and feminine energy* was used because for decades it was a simple and effective shorthand to help people understand the concepts of *projective and active* vs. *passive and receptive* energy binaries. This example, and other outdated descriptors, may not resonate with today's audiences, but Qabala is so much more than the metaphors that have been used to describe it. The study of Qabala is ever unfolding, and with every generation, our comprehension of it deepens and expands. While those working on the Tree of Life before us overlaid it with problematic explanations and metaphors, the power of the Tree transcends those interpretations and opens itself to modern ways of thinking.

....

1. Misha Magdalene, *Outside the Charmed Circle: Exploring Gender & Sexuality in Magical Practice* (Woodbury, MN: Llewellyn Publications, 2020), 33–34.

One of the goals of this book is to closely examine existing metaphors used to explain Qabala to find the queerness within, as well as create some new metaphors to make Qabala friendlier to a queer audience. In this book, you'll find queer-inclusive pathworkings, exercises, and spells to connect you with this powerful, magickal tool.

Another goal of this book is to provide a simple, approachable introduction to Qabala. Qabala study can be overwhelming! Many of the introductory books put a lot of focus on complex charts, lists, and tables of correspondences. While there will be a few correspondence charts in this book, I keep them to a minimum. In determining what should be covered in this book, I used a filter of "What is the most useful thing to know to help someone connect to this concept?" I focused on the core of a concept and worked to make it relatable and understandable. While Qabala is a tool that invites deep research, in this book my aim is to help you build a personal connection with the Tree of Life rather than an encyclopedic knowledge of it.

Who Is This Book For?

If you've picked this book up off the shelf or are scanning the introduction online, this book is for you. Whether you are a Qabala newbie or an expert, whether you are queer or an ally, welcome. In this book you'll find a grounded introduction to the basics of Qabala, opportunities to expand your viewpoint on Qabala, and practical tips for queering your magickal practice.

If you are an ally, trying to be an ally, or have a deeply embedded knowledge of Qabala, I encourage you to take the following perspective while reading this book: What you know is yours, and your lived experience is your truth. When this book focuses on perspectives or ideas that are different from your experiences and you find yourself feeling alienated, pay attention. In addition to this experience mirroring what queer folks go through with most books, these are probably ideas that will lead to new and more expansive perspectives for you and are worth contemplation.

In the interest of transparency, I will note that my Pagan spiritual background is primarily in Wicca and ceremonial magick, though my intent is for this book to be applicable and useful in a wide array of magickal practices. If examples from my spiritual background don't resonate with you, I encourage you to think of a corollary within your own spiritual practice.

What Does This Book Hope to Accomplish?

If you want two key takeaways from this book, they are: 1. Qabala is a powerful magickal tool fit for modern magickal practitioners of all sexualities and genders, and 2. Qabala is already queer, and we can make it even more so. Through a friendly, simplified, easy-to-connect-with, and extremely queer introduction to the Tree of Life, I want to help queer people see themselves in Qabala and help Qabala teachers of all sexualities and genders to be more inclusive in their teaching methods. Qabala, after all, is supposed to represent the entirety of the universe and the full range of human experience. There are aspects of the Tree of Life that become easier to see when you shift your perspective.

Expanding perspectives in teaching is particularly important because despite the fact that many Pagan and magickal communities pride themselves on being open and welcoming to a variety of genders and sexualities, the language and symbolism we use in many of our rituals are cisheteronormative. *Cisheteronormative* means *embracing traditional male and female gender roles relating to birth sex and the assumption of heterosexuality as the norm.*[2] When someone describes how magick works with metaphors related to stereotypical gender roles and heterosexual intercourse, for example, it makes it harder for queer people to see ourselves and our lived experiences in the magick. We'll get deeper into this in chapter 2.

Magickal communities are traditions that, by their nature, draw people on the fringes of society. It's therefore imperative we continually reexamine our language, symbols, assumptions, and structures to see

. . . .
2. Morgan Lev Edward Holleb, *The A-Z of Gender and Sexuality: From Ace to Ze* (London: Jessica Kingsley Publishers, 2019), 70–71.

where they might be alienating for people who have too long been under-represented and misrepresented in mainstream culture. We are called to social justice and greater inclusivity, and reexamining how we teach and practice through different lenses is part of that. If queer people are coming to Pagan traditions in search of authenticity and empowerment, the worst thing we can do is dampen that spirit by keeping to rigid, binary structures for the sake of tradition or because of lack of creativity on our part.

It is our job, as Pagans and magickal practitioners, not only to welcome queer people into magickal spaces, but also to affirm them and help them blossom into the most amazing queer people they can be. Let's stop telling people they can come into a premade space and find their own home in it with the way it's already set up. Instead, let's co-create spaces that make everyone feel empowered and connected.

How and Why I Use the Word *Queer*

In this book, I use the word *queer* in a few ways. I often use it as a catch-all adjective: an umbrella description for those who are not heterosexual, cisgender (identifying with the sex they were assigned at birth), or heteroromantic (exclusively romantically interested in a binary gender different from their own). This includes lesbian, gay, bisexual, transgender, nonbinary, queer, questioning, intersex, asexual, pansexual, and two-spirit individuals, as well as others with non-cisgender, non-heteroromantic, non-heterosexual identities.[3]

I occasionally use *queer* as a verb. *To queer* something means to view it through a lens that calls into question anything we take for granted as normal: particularly binary, cisheteronormative ways of thinking.[4]

Some people find the word *queer* objectionable, so I want to take a minute to explain why I use it.

. . . .

3. Daniel Villarreal, "What Does Queer Mean? Well, There's No One Definition." LGBTQ Nation, September 21, 2019, https://www.lgbtqnation.com/2019/09/queer-mean-well -theres-no-one-definition/.

4. Holleb, *The A-Z of Gender and Sexuality*, 211, 214–16.

First, *queer* is quicker and easier to scan, and more all-encompassing than the various acronyms used to describe the queer community, including LGBT, LGBTQIAP2S, and variations in between. The letters in these acronyms stand for lesbian, gay, bisexual, transgender, queer/questioning, intersex, asexual/aromantic, pansexual, and two-spirit. Sometimes a plus sign (+) is added to the end of the acronym to acknowledge the fact that these words do not comprehensively represent the queer community; though that, too, can be alienating for those whose identities aren't included in the acronym. After all, who wants their identity relegated to a plus sign? I use *queer* instead of these acronyms because our understanding of the various identities within the umbrella of non-cisheteronormativity is constantly evolving and expanding, which is a wonderful thing!

Second, using *queer* is a nod to the academic discipline of queer theory, which takes a critical eye to cisheteronormativity. The fact that *queer* has been used to describe university and postgraduate courses and degrees since the 1990s shows how incredibly mainstream the term's usage has become.[5]

Third, I reject the notion that words that have been used as slurs should never be used as community or personal identity labels. People in queer and other civil rights movements have a long, proud history of reclaiming words used against us by our oppressors. We have been reclaiming the word *queer* since the 1980s.[6] The term *gay* has been a slur for decades in the United States too, but there isn't the same backlash against the word *gay* as there is for the word *queer*. And there's a reason for that.

Unfortunately, much of this backlash to the word *queer* is manufactured and stoked by people who wish to divide the queer community, not unite it—people who don't like the B and T, much less the letters that follow, included in the acronym LGBTQIAP2S+. For example, a media

. . . .

5. Meg-John Barker and Jules Scheele, *Queer: A Graphic History* (London: Icon Books Ltd., 2016), 59.

6. Barker and Scheele, *Queer: A Graphic History*, 10.

style guide released by anti-trans group, the Women's Liberation Front, specifically says not to use the word *queer* because it's a slur.[7]

While the LGBTQIAP2S acronym and its variations have the potential to unite us under a common umbrella, they can also be used to divide us. The identifiers that appear after the L and the G are less likely to be the face of our community in the media, at Pride, and in critical conversations. As a result, bisexuals, transgender people, nonbinary people, intersex people, asexuals, pansexuals, two-spirit people, and others in the queer community often get left out of community spaces.

When I use *queer* in this book, it is in acknowledgment that while our struggles may not always be the same, the queer umbrella is big enough for everyone in the LGBTQIAP2S community, even those whose letters haven't been added to the acronym yet. By using *queer* to describe the community, I acknowledge our community contains a wide array of non-cisgender and non-heterosexual people, including people whose identities are in flux, uncertain, or don't yet have a comfortable label.

I also realize, however, that for some, it is difficult to read words that have been hurled against you by your oppressors, and in some parts of the world, *queer* is still used almost exclusively as a slur. I have compassion for those against whom the term is routinely weaponized, and I believe nobody should be forced to use the term as a personal identifier, even as I advocate for its use as a catchall term in our community.

To that end, I want to prescribe a bit of caution to others, particularly cisgender heterosexual people, in using this term. If you're using this term in a casual way to describe the community, use it as an adjective rather than a noun—*queer people* or *the queer community* as opposed to *queers*. If you're considering using this term to describe someone's gender or sexual identity, ensure that person is comfortable using that word to describe themself. If they describe themself as bisexual, transgender, gay, lesbian, etc., use those words instead of *queer*. Just as we must always respect someone's pronouns, we must also respect how a person chooses

. . . .

7. "WoLF Media Style Guide," accessed December 29, 2020, https://www.womens
liberationfront.org/news/wolf-media-style-guide.

to describe themself, and not everyone is comfortable describing themselves as *queer*, even if they consider themselves members of the *queer community*.

While it is wise to routinely put language under the microscope, to prod terms to see if they are still the best terms to serve our needs, thus far I have not seen a better word than *queer* to succinctly and inclusively describe our community. When a new, all-encompassing term is agreed upon to replace *queer*, I'll happily embrace it. But for the purposes of this book, *queer* is the word, and Qabala is queer.

A Note on Cultural Appropriation

Speaking of ongoing cultural conversations, I want to take a moment to discuss cultural appropriation, which sometimes comes up in conversations about Hermetic Qabala.

Cultural appropriation is a form of colonization: it is when a more-privileged culture co-opts an oppressed culture's identity markers, usually without acknowledgment of the source. Another definition, more tailored for magickal practitioners, written by Thumper Forge, is: "Cultural appropriation occurs when a minority practice is adopted by the members of a majority, who then a) deny the minority access to that practice, or b) condemn the minority for continuing to engage in the practice."[8]

The idea of cultural appropriation shares some overlap with the idea of *closed practices*: secret practices only taught to initiates within a spiritual tradition or practices of a particular culture that are not intended to be studied or practiced by people outside that culture. Someone outside a particular culture profiting off a closed practice would be one form of cultural appropriation.

· · · · · · · · · · · · · · · ·

8. Thumper Forge, "Cancelled for Renovations: More Thoughts on Closed Practices." *Fivefold Law* (blog), Patheos, May 19, 2021, https://www.patheos.com/blogs/fivefoldlaw/2021/05/19/cancelled-for-renovations-more-thoughts-on-closed-practices/.

Hermetic Qabala, the subject of this book, is an open practice and can be studied by occultists from any faith background.[9] The Jewish devotional practice of Kabbalah, however, is understood to be a closed practice within the Jewish community and is not the subject of this book.

Hermetic Qabala has its roots in the Jewish study of Kabbalah, which itself was influenced by Ancient Greek and Roman philosophy as well as lore and concepts from the "Chaldeans, the pre-Aryan Indians, the Greeks, and other Semitic people in the Middle East."[10] What we know today as Hermetic Qabala is a distinct approach to the Tree of Life, one that has been developed, often in collaboration with Jewish scholars, for hundreds of years.[11] The Jewish devotional practice of Kabbalah is focused on the ten aspects of the divine god. The occult practice of Qabala is focused on levels of consciousness, magickal systems, and the inner and outer landscapes. The two practices share some components in common—the Tree of Life glyph, Hebrew names of spheres, and Hebrew letters on the paths, for example—but have completely different approaches to and uses for the same spiritual tool.

If I, a non-Jew, were to tell you that I know a better way to approach the Jewish devotional practice of Kabbalah, that would be cultural appropriation. I'm not going to do that. In this book, I will be staying in my lane as a Hermetic Qabalist and only mentioning Jewish Kabbalah where it's relevant to discuss the historical roots of Hermetic Qabala.

All that said, I have a lot of thoughts on Hermetic Qabala, and I am excited to share them with you.

How to Use This Book

This book is broken into three parts.

In part 1, you'll get an introduction to Qabala, learn what makes it an excellent queer magickal tool, and dig into concepts of queer magickal

. . . .

9. Israel Regardie, *A Garden of Pomegranates: An Outline of the Qabalah* (Los Angeles: New Falcon, 2019), xxii.
10. Christopher Penczak, *The Temple of High Witchcraft: Ceremonies, Spheres, and the Witches' Qabalah* (Woodbury, MN: Llewellyn Publications, 2017), 84.
11. Penczak, *The Temple of High Witchcraft*, 84.

practice in general, including polarity as it pertains to magick. Exercises in this section will help you connect with the Tree of Life as a whole and embrace queerness as an authentic component of magickal practice, regardless of whether you are queer or an ally.

In part 2, you'll gain a deeper understanding of the individual spheres, or sephiroth, from a queer perspective. Each sphere's section includes at least one exercise to consider the sphere's impact on your life. Most of these are labeled as journaling exercises, but I know journaling isn't for everyone. Any place where I recommend you journal your thoughts, I also offer alternatives, such as recording yourself speaking instead. The point is to spend time thinking and considering and to get those thoughts outside your head in some way. In addition to the exercises, I've also included pathworkings for each of the spheres. While the pathworkings aren't specifically queer, I've taken care to ensure the experiences are as gender- and sexuality-neutral as possible so you can bring your own perspective to bear. I include these exercises and pathworkings because the Qabala must be felt and experienced, not just intellectually understood. I recommend taking some time after each chapter in part 2 to allow yourself to integrate what you've learned rather than rushing to read the next chapter immediately.

In part 3, you'll find a variety of queer magickal workings using the Qabala as a framework. These workings range in complexity from *very simple, no tools required, and takes only a few minutes* to *you will need to buy some stuff for this working, and it could take a few months to complete.* In addition to experiencing Qabala through pathworkings, another important way to learn Qabala is to use it, and these workings will give you the opportunity to do so.

How to Use the Pathworkings in This Book

The pathworkings in this book are guided meditations to introduce you to the concepts of Qabala in an experiential way. While surrendering to the experience is certainly part of experiencing a pathworking, you are in control of what you do and what happens, and what you experience may be different from what I have written. That's okay! You're also welcome to end the pathworking at any time if you feel it's too intense or you just aren't in the right headspace for it at that moment.

I recommend skimming each pathworking before you experience it so you have a rough idea what it contains. If there are aspects of the pathworking that make you uncomfortable, feel free to change them, divert course, or ignore them. This is your experience, and you are in control. I'll remind you of this at the beginning of each pathworking in the book.

You may approach the pathworkings in this book in whichever way works best for you:

1. Read them to yourself, then close your eyes and attempt the journey based on your memory of what you've read.

2. Record yourself reading them out loud, then play them back as you follow them.

3. Ask a friend to read them aloud to you.

I recommend keeping a journal or recording device nearby when doing the pathworkings so you can write, draw, or record yourself speaking about your experiences immediately afterward. Details of magickal experiences tend to fade quickly, so it's helpful to record them to reflect upon later.

PART 1

Introduction to Queer Qabala

W hat is Qabala, and what makes it queer? To answer these questions, we'll start with the basic building blocks of Qabala: its history, the symbols it contains, and its relationship to other magickal systems. We'll establish a common understanding of the concept of polarity in magickal practice as an entry point for considering ways to queer your practice.

Once we've laid that groundwork, we'll dig into the concepts of queerness and magick, and then how queer gender and sexuality are represented in Qabala in all their complexity.

What Is Qabala?

Qabala is a framework for understanding and experiencing "Life, the Universe, and Everything"—to quote sci-fi author Douglas Adams wildly out of context.[12] It is a tool for elevating consciousness, for deepening your understanding of yourself, and for discovering and embracing the whole of manifested and unmanifested reality.

History of Qabala

Qabala's roots are in the Jewish tradition, though the Tree of Life has also been studied by Christians and occult mystics for centuries.[13] The word *Qabala* or *Kabbalah* originates from the Hebrew letters Qoph (or Koph) Beth Lamed, which together mean *received, oral tradition,* or *tradition.*[14] The word is typically, though not universally, spelled with a Q when referring to Hermetic Qabala and with a K, *Kabbalah,* when referring to the Jewish devotional practice.

. . . .

12. Douglas Adams, *The Hitchhiker's Guide to the Galaxy* (New York: Harmony Books, 2000), 129.

13. Regardie, *A Garden of Pomegranates,* 2; Penczak, *The Temple of High Witchcraft,* 84.

14. Penczak, *The Temple of High Witchcraft,* 82.

But where did the Tree of Life come from? We don't actually know. There's a mythic history saying the Tree of Life was gifted by angels to either Adam in the Garden of Eden or to Moses atop Mount Sinai. Some scholars suspect Moses, raised in the Egyptian court, may have learned or developed Kabbalah in collaboration with Egyptian priests.[15] These theories are fun to consider, but we have no historical evidence of their truth.

In terms of written tradition, the *Sepher Yetzirah* (Book of Formation), which introduced the concept of the ten spheres, originates between 100 and 900 CE.[16] Study of the spheres and what became known as the Tree of Life continued into the Middle Ages. In the eleventh century, scholars began to incorporate concepts from the works of Plato and other ancient Greek philosophers into Kabbalah.[17] In the Renaissance, Spain was an epicenter of mystical study and thought, and scholars believe that Jewish and non-Jewish mystics and scholars shared knowledge of Kabbalah there.[18] The Tree of Life glyph we use today was first published in 1652, though there were several competing models at the time.[19]

In the late 1800s, the Hermetic Order of the Golden Dawn was founded, and they produced a great deal of scholarship around the mystical aspects of Qabala. The Order was a major force in the Western Mystery Tradition, which is "a broad set of esoteric disciplines rooted in magickal and mystical practices" drawing heavily from Greek and Egyptian mystery schools.[20] Israel Regardie, who was raised Jewish, was a key player in preserving, sharing, and publishing the Order's teachings, including those on Qabala, which had a powerful shaping influence on modern Paganism and magick.

. . . .

15. Robert Wang, *The Qabalistic Tarot, A Textbook of Mystical Philosophy* (York Beach, ME: Weiser Books, 1983), 5; Ellen Cannon Reed, *The Witches Qabala: The Pagan Path and the Tree of Life* (Boston: Weiser Books, 1997), 5.

16. Penczak, *The Temple of High Witchcraft*, 84.

17. Regardie, *A Garden of Pomegranates*, 3; Penczak, *The Temple of High Witchcraft*, 84.

18. Penczak, *The Temple of High Witchcraft*, 84.

19. Wang, *The Qabalistic Tarot*, 31.

20. Daniel Moler, *Shamanic Qabalah: A Mystical Path to Uniting the Tree of Life & the Great Work* (Woodbury, MN: Llewellyn Publications, 2018), 5.

What Is the Tree of Life?

The Tree of Life is a diagram, or glyph, that is core to the study of Qabala and Kabbalah. The glyph shows ten circles, also known as sephiroth (the plural of sephira) or spheres, connected by twenty-two lines, also known as paths. Each sphere and path is assigned a number, and each path is assigned

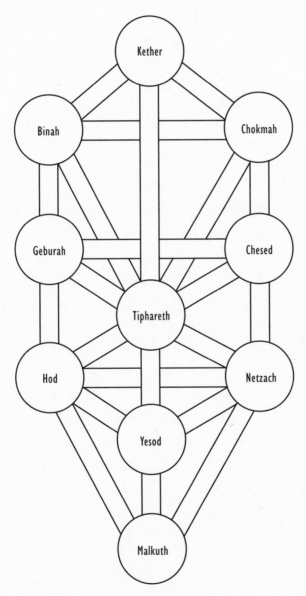

Figure 1: The Tree of Life

a corresponding letter in the Hebrew alphabet. The spheres are also considered paths, giving us thirty-two paths in total. The spheres represent static concepts, states of being, and levels of consciousness, whereas the paths represent the transformative experience of moving between those states. The arrangement of paths and spheres into the Tree of Life glyph is a kind of "spiritual architecture," as Qabalist Daniel Moler puts it.[21]

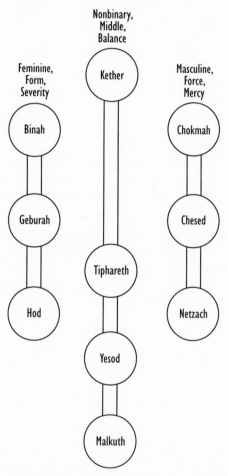

Figure 2: The three pillars on the Tree of Life

The glyph shows three vertical lines, or pillars. Each pillar is known by multiple names. From left to right, the pillars are the Feminine Pillar, also known as the Pillar of Form or Pillar of Severity; the Middle Pillar, also

21. Moler, *Shamanic Qabalah*, 3.

known as the Pillar of Balance; and the Masculine Pillar, also known as the Pillar of Force or Pillar of Mercy. For the purposes of this book, I will be referring to these as the Pillars of Form, Balance, and Force unless I'm making a particular point about gender, in which case I'll refer to them as the Feminine Pillar, the Nonbinary Pillar, and the Masculine Pillar.

The top of the Tree is where the most abstract concepts of force, form, and unity are located. The very bottom of the Tree represents manifestation: our tangible, lived reality on this plane. For those who work with the concept of vibrations, the highest part of the Tree can be thought of as having a very high vibration, and the bottom of the Tree a much lower vibration, representing the densest concentration of energy, including that which we know as *matter.*

From a mystical perspective, the Tree of Life describes many things, including humanity's relationship with divinity, the manner in which things become manifest, a map for a personal growth journey, different levels of consciousness, and a "filing cabinet of the universe"—a descriptor Ellen Cannon Reed paraphrased from Israel Regardie.[22] The glyph also acts as a key for obtaining knowledge and experiences via meditation and pathworkings, and serves as a composite symbol representing the interrelationships between various magickal systems, like astrology and tarot.

I know that sounds like a lot, and it is. Qabala is *everything*. So let's break that down a bit.

Map of Personal Growth

One of the more frustrating things about a quest to align yourself with your higher purpose is the lack of clear progress indicators. Qabala is wonderful in that it offers a map of the progress of one's personal growth or spiritual evolution. As Israel Regardie said, "The Qabala is a trustworthy guide, leading to a comprehension both of the Universe and one's own Self."[23]

The spheres describe everything in the universe, and they also describe the universe that exists inside each person. Many Pagans adhere to the belief of "As above, so below, but in a different manner," and to that end, everything is a microcosm of the larger cosmos. We each have a Tree of

....
22. Reed, *Witches Qabala*, 3; Regardie, *A Garden of Pomegranates*, 27.
23. Regardie, *A Garden of Pomegranates*, xxii.

Life within us, and the Tree describes not only distinct parts of our self, but also our connection with the infinite.

The spheres represent different archetypes, each a step between our mundane existence and unity with the infinite. As we grow spiritually, as we connect with different aspects of our consciousness, we begin to understand the Tree of Life within us. In part 2 of this book, I will help you awaken the spheres within.

Everything Is Divine

For those of us raised in faiths where we were taught that we could not access God except through intermediaries of clergy, one of the biggest draws of Paganism is the idea of divinity not being separate from our day-to-day life. And while some may think the Qabala demonstrates a separation of humanity and divinity, that is only a surface view. In fact, the Tree of Life shows us that divinity is in everything and that there is no area of life or experience untouched by infinite, divine energy.

Mainstream American and European cultures often teach that the concepts of good and divine are all about light, love, creation, and joy; but in Qabalistic teaching, everything is divine, even that which limits and that which destroys. Equal weight is given to force and form as well as creation and destruction, and it makes sense why: We can't go around creating things endlessly—we'd run out of room. There's beauty and divinity in decomposition, in digestion, in death, in healthy limitations that help us grow into our best selves. All that exists passes through all the spheres of the Tree on its way to manifestation.

Pathway into Manifestation: The Lightning Flash

If you play connect-the-dots with the Tree glyph, drawing straight lines between each of the spheres in the order in which they came into being, you will get the Lightning Flash, a pictorial view of how energy flows down the tree. It starts at Kether, the first sphere to come into existence, and ends in Malkuth, the tenth and final sphere to come into existence.

The Lightning Flash tells the story of the creation of the universe, and it is useful for helping us understand the pathway energy follows from nothingness into manifestation today.

It starts by passing through three veils that exist before Kether, the first sphere. These veils are Ain, Ain Soph, and Air Soph Aur, which roughly translate to "nothing," "limitless nothing," and "limitless light." You can think of it as a sort of story: There was absolute nothing (Ain), and then the nothingness realized it was nothingness (Ain Soph), and then the nothingness realized that its nothingness was actually a thing in itself (Ain Soph Aur). Qabalist Robin Fennelly describes these as "the stimulation, urge, and subsequent action" toward Kether, the first sphere.[24]

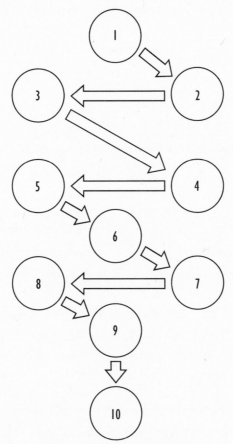

Figure 3: The Lightning Flash

24. Robin Fennelly, *The Inner Chamber, Volume 2: Poetry of the Spheres, Qabala* (Philadelphia: Robin Fennelly, 2012), 175.

From Kether, the sphere of raw potential, this energy passes into Chokmah, the sphere of endless energy, then Binah, which gives it the potential for form, followed by Chesed, where it can begin to envision what that form could be. Then Geburah edits that concept down to something that's at home in Tiphareth, the sphere of balance, followed by Netzach, where that energy gets split into its component pieces, which are then named in Hod. Then the energy passes through the final editor of Yesod, where it takes on its final form before becoming manifest in Malkuth. This process and these spheres will all be covered at length later in this book.

Working with the Lightning Flash helps magickal practitioners manifest our Will. Understanding the steps energy flows through in order to become manifest is key to making our Will manifest on this plane. Acknowledging and working with this energy flow while doing magickal work is like paddling with, rather than against, the current of a river: it makes your work easier.

What does a journey down the Lightning Flash feel like? I wrote this very short story to describe it:

> *Once upon a time, before there was time, there was nothing but potential. That potential was contained into one, impossibly small, bright dot.*
>
> *Then something happened, and the dot began to expand. And for a while, that was all it did and all it could do: rush out in every direction, limitless and excited to move.*
>
> *But energy without direction can't do anything, and so that energy began to take shape. With shape, all things became possible, including beginnings and endings.*

Time began, and with it, the concepts of creation and life.

But the universe couldn't just create life and things endlessly. It needed the concept of breaking down—it needed a metabolism to digest itself, to remove and recycle excesses —and with that concept came the potential for balance. The universe realized that all things could not be all at once in every way. Each thing needed limits and to sacrifice potential in order to evolve into its own unique purpose.

And seeing its potential for all these unique things, the universe fell deeply, completely, wildly, passionately in love with itself, and in that love it started to truly see all the possibilities and to give them all names so that they could live together and celebrate their differences and similarities, first in the land of imagination, and then finally to be born into existence on this plane, where they could live, die, create, destroy, find balance, love, study, imagine, and be.

The Lightning Flash, when traveled in reverse, offers us the most complete route for raising our consciousness beyond manifest reality in the quest to touch the source of all. We travel the Lightning Flash in reverse in our meditations to achieve new levels of consciousness, and will do so in part 2, where we begin our journey in Malkuth. In my experience, it's easier to understand the concepts of the more ephemeral spheres when we begin with our roots and work our way up.

The Three Triangles

Qabalists divide the glyph into three triangles: The first consisting of Kether, Chokmah, and Binah; the second consisting of Chesed, Geburah, and Tiphareth; and the third consisting of Netzach, Hod, and Yesod. Each of these triangles can be thought of as a different evolutionary phase, different aspects of the spirit, or different parts of self.

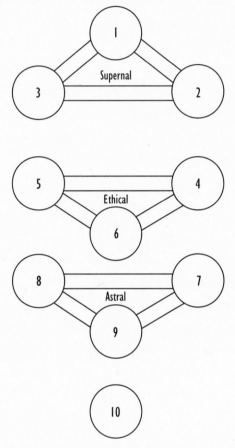

Figure 4: The triangles within the Tree of Life (traditional)

The first triangle is traditionally called the Supernal Triangle and includes spiritual concepts that exist beyond form but represent the building blocks that make manifestation possible.

The second triangle is called the Ethical Triangle, Moral Triangle, or Mental Triangle. The spheres in this triangle represent mystical consciousness and are an early testing ground for energies on their way to manifestation.

The third triangle is called the Astral Triangle or Psychic Triangle and represents "human levels of consciousness"[25] and the final editorial processes that occur before manifestation. These are the spheres closest to our daily reality.

Malkuth is the only sphere that isn't part of a triangle because it *is* our daily reality.

You can think of these triangles as representing the spirit, the soul, and the personality, respectively, or the higher, middle, and lower selves. The organization of the Tree into these triangles demonstrates that raising our consciousness is not the same as climbing a ladder; it's a constant process of mentally understanding and spiritually experiencing the concepts of force and form, while holding a strong sense of central balance throughout.

What does that mean? Well, I'll explain with a metaphor: One of my favorite hobbies is indoor rock climbing. Many people assume that climbing requires significant upper body strength, but really, core strength and a flexible sense of balance are more important. I think of it as *vertical dancing* because you're in a constant state of flow between different points of balance. Sometimes the point of balance that is available looks very unbalanced from below: you may need to perch on one toe while leaning way over to one side before you can reach your next foot- or handhold. As you move, you typically have two or three points of your body—a combination of hands and feet—on the wall and one point moving to the next hold. The keys to climbing successfully are being able to freely flow your balance between feet and hands, between left and right, and being able to hold your weight on a very small point while keeping your body close to the wall and remembering to breathe.

In the same way, ascending the Tree of Life requires you to lean more in the direction of form at times and more in the direction of force at other times, but the important thing is to remain in balance as you explore. As you keep two or three points of your body on the climbing wall for stability, so, too, will understanding the spheres in the context of

25. Penczak, *The Temple of High Witchcraft*, 144.

their triangle help you create a balanced understanding of the forces of the Tree.

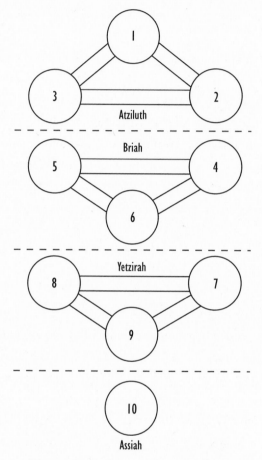

Figure 5: The four worlds (one option)

The Four Worlds: Oh My God … It's Full of Trees

Earlier, when I talked about how the Tree of Life contains everything in the universe and yet there is also a Tree of Life within you, I mentioned a key premise to understanding Qabala: patterns on a large scale are reflected on a small scale and vice versa, and you can influence the world and gain wisdom through working with those connections. It's helpful for me to think of these universal patterns as a huge fractal: an infinite pattern that looks exactly the same no matter how closely you zoom in on it.

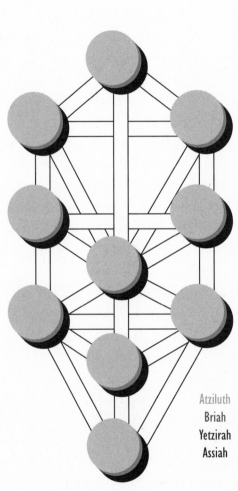

Atziluth
Briah
Yetzirah
Assiah

Figure 6: The four worlds (another option)

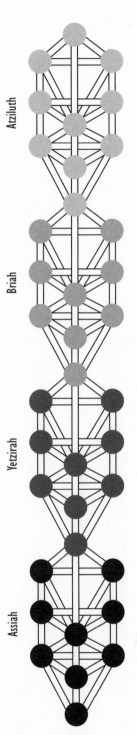

Atziluth

Briah

Yetzirah

Assiah

Figure 7: The four worlds
(yet another option)

As the Tree of Life reflects the universe as a whole, it is basically one giant fractal too. There are Trees within Trees and Trees existing on multiple planes of existence.

In Qabala, we acknowledge four worlds, or dimensions. These worlds are called Atziluth, Briah, Yetzirah, and Assiah, and they represent, on a macro level, the creation process. Atziluth represents the spark. Briah represents creation. Yetzirah represents the form. Assiah represents that which is manifested. Most magickal work takes place in Briah and Yetzirah before becoming manifested in Assiah. To that end, my discussion of the Tree in this book doesn't focus on its form in Atziluth, since Atziluth is simply too ephemeral for words to encompass.

There are different ways to view these four worlds. They can be overlaid upon the Tree of Life, with Malkuth itself being Assiah; the triangle of Yesod, Hod, and Netzach being Yetzirah; the triangle of Tiphareth, Geburah, and Chesed being Briah; and the triangle of Binah, Chokmah, and Kether being Atziluth. I particularly like this version of the four worlds because it mirrors the way in which the Lightning Flash already represents different phases of creation.

Alternatively, the four worlds are viewed as having their own individual Trees, existing on different planes but in relationship with each other. The trees could be layered over each other, with each sphere stacked atop its corresponding spheres in the other worlds, similarly to how some describe parallel universes coexisting. This is a useful model for when you want to work with the four worlds of a particular sphere: rising on the planes of existence from Assiah to Yetzirah, but staying in Yesod, for example.

You can also view the four worlds stacked in a different way, where each Tree's Kether is the next Tree's Malkuth. This model makes sense if you're trying to explain the story of creation on a grander scale.

Adding to this complex picture, each sphere contains its own Tree of Life. Many magickal practitioners are accustomed to the nuances of elemental combinations: working with the air of water, as an example. Qabala works in a similar way—there's a Tiphareth of Geburah, a Chesed of Netzach, and so on. Much of our initial work with the Tree of Life may actually be limited to the Tree within Malkuth, which encompasses our material existence and is therefore easier to comprehend.

Simply put: The Tree of Life is a fractal. Every aspect of the Tree is represented in every other aspect of the Tree. All is one; one is all. It is both infinitely complex and infinitely simple. In learning about the whole Tree, you are also deepening your understanding of its components and vice versa.

The Paths

When you look at the Tree of Life glyph, you see twenty-two lines connecting ten spheres. You can think of the spheres as pools of energy and the paths as streams connecting them, or you could think of the spheres as cities, connected by roads representing the paths.

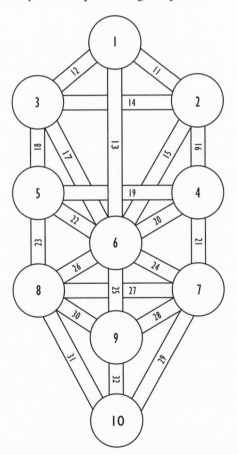

Figure 8: The paths on the Tree of Life

The quick-and-dirty explanation of the paths is that the paths represent the subjective, transformative experience of moving between the objective states of being that are represented by the spheres. There is a huge amount of nuance to that, of course, as both the spheres and the paths offer the opportunity for personal experience and self-discovery. The experience of the paths, however, tends to be much more highly individualized. The paths are an excellent tool for what many magickal workers call *shadow work*, or uncovering the darker parts of our psyche and understanding them better so they no longer control us.

Each path is associated with one of the twenty-two letters of the Hebrew alphabet. Each letter is encoded with mathematical and linguistic mysteries, representing twenty-two aspects of the powers of creation. Please see the further reading section on page 219 for some recommended books on the paths and the Hebrew letters associated with each.

There are also hidden paths not represented on the glyph. A hidden path is a straight-line connection between two spheres that *isn't* a line shown on the Tree of Life glyph. One of these paths is part of the Lightning Flash: the journey between the third and fourth spheres: Binah and Chesed.

The hidden paths can be traveled through journey work, just like the other, not-hidden paths. However, they are very intense experiences and are not appropriate for study in an introductory Qabala practice. Work with the twenty-two paths in the glyph first, get comfortable with them, and then, if you're interested, do some research to learn more about the hidden paths.

Filing Cabinet of the Universe/Correspondences

One of the metaphors for describing the Tree of Life, paraphrasing Israel Regardie, is *a filing cabinet for the universe.*[26] Everything we can conceive of fits somewhere in the Tree.

If you think about a filing cabinet in the mundane world, it serves two purposes: for organizing things and for retrieving them based on that

....
26. Reed, *Witches Qabala,* 3; Regardie, *A Garden of Pomegranates,* 27.

organization. Scholars have spent centuries "filing" information about various things in the universe in the Tree of Life, and Qabalists have the opportunity to access this information through building a deep connection with the Tree. Understanding the Tree of Life and building a relationship with it can be the key to understanding other magickal systems as well.

One of the points I'll repeat throughout this book is that it's incumbent upon all Qabalists to add to and deepen our understanding of the Tree of Life. In the words of Daniel Moler, "It is powered by those who have previously worked it throughout history, but it is up to us to take that knowledge and move it forward."[27] You have the opportunity to add things to that filing cabinet that could one day be accessed by future generations: like an eternal, spiritual World Wide Web.

Many Qabala books include charts of the things scholars have already "filed" in the Tree: each sphere has an assigned virtue, vice, illusion, spiritual experience, archangel, and choir of angels, and scholars have also added to each sphere specific plants, crystals, deities, fragrances, days of the week, and more. When I was first learning Qabala, I found these charts more intimidating than immediately useful. If you want to dig deeper into these correspondences, I invite you to check out the recommended books in the further reading section (page 219). I'm only including two charts in this book with particularly useful correspondences for many magickal practitioners: tarot and astrology. If you're already conversant in one or both of these systems, it'll make understanding Qabala that much easier. Understanding how these three systems interconnect will benefit your magickal practice. For each system you work with, you will deepen your understanding of the other two systems.

Tarot

Qabala is the operating system of most modern tarot decks. Mathematically, it works out very neatly: There are twenty-two cards in the major arcana and twenty-two paths connecting the spheres on the Tree of Life.

....
27. Moler, *Shamanic Qabalah*, 3.

The minor arcana consists of the numbers one through ten, and there are ten spheres on the Tree. There are four designations of court cards, and there are four worlds of the Tree.

In an interesting and counterintuitive twist, the paths between spheres in the Tree of Life are associated with the cards in the major arcana of the tarot, and the spheres are associated with the cards in the minor arcana. It seems weird at first—shouldn't the spheres, the most prominent aspects of the Tree, be associated with the big events of the major arcana? But it makes sense when you think more deeply about it. The spheres represent more static states of being, whereas the paths represent the process of moving between those states. In much the same way, the cards of the minor arcana represent snapshots of life, and the major arcana cards depict the Fool's journey: the process of spiritual evolution.

As for the court cards (pages, knights, queens, and kings in the Rider-Waite-Smith deck), they represent their element within each of the four worlds: the court cards in the pentacles suit, for example, represent the element of earth as it is expressed in Atzliuth, Briah, Yetzirah, and Assiah. There are different schools of thought as to which court card represents which of the four worlds, and I'm not going to belabor that debate here. The construct I see most often is the court cards representing the path to manifestation: pages represent the spark of something beginning (Atziluth), knights represent the work to get things moving in the right direction (Briah), queens represent a near-complete state (Yetzirah), and kings represent the finished product, the manifested reality (Assiah). This approach is fairly patriarchal, however, and speaks to one of the flaws of the Rider-Waite-Smith deck structure in describing kings as more complete or more powerful than queens. I encourage you to consider queering the cards in a way that works for you, and recommend reading *Queering the Tarot* by Cassandra Snow to get deeper into that subject.

The Major Arcana	Path
The Fool	11: Kether to Chokmah
The Magician	12: Kether to Binah
The High Priestess	13: Kether to Tiphareth
The Empress	14: Chokmah to Binah
The Emperor	15: Chokmah to Tiphareth
The Hierophant	16: Chokmah to Chesed
The Lovers	17 Binah to Tiphareth
The Chariot	18: Binah to Geburah
Strength	19: Chesed to Geburah
The Hermit	20: Chesed to Tiphareth
The Wheel of Fortune	21: Chesed to Netzach
Justice	22: Geburah to Tiphareth
The Hanged Man	23: Geburah to Hod
Death	24: Tiphareth to Netzach
Temperance	25: Tiphareth to Yesod
The Devil	26: Tiphareth to Hod
The Tower	27: Netzach to Hod
The Star	28: Netzach to Yesod
The Moon	29: Netzach to Malkuth
The Sun	30: Hod to Yesod
Judgement	31: Hod to Malkuth
The World	32: Yesod to Malkuth

The Minor Arcana	Sphere
Aces	Kether
Twos	Chokmah
Threes	Binah
Fours	Chesed
Fives	Geburah
Sixes	Tiphareth
Sevens	Netzach
Eights	Hod
Nines	Yesod
Tens	Malkuth

How can you use Qabala correspondences in tarot? For me, learning Qabala added another layer of interpretation to my tarot readings. When I'm struggling to determine what a particular card means within a spread, if the image itself isn't speaking to me that day, I will recall its corresponding sphere or path within the Tree of Life, and that always helps me sort its meaning.

If you build an altar devoted to a particular sphere, you can include its corresponding minor arcana cards and contemplate how they represent that sphere.

Tarot can also teach you more about Qabala. If you're trying to better understand a sphere or path, examine its corresponding tarot card(s). You can also use cards as portals to journey into spheres and paths. Some excellent books have been written on this subject. You'll find them in the further reading section (page 219).

Astrology

Similarly to tarot, an understanding of astrology will aid in your understanding of Qabala and vice versa. Each sphere and path corresponds to a planet, an element, or an astrological sign.

Unlike with tarot, the math on the spheres and paths vs. their various correspondences in astrology isn't quite as tidy. This is understandable, since we've discovered new planets since the Tree of Life glyph was designed. The spheres correspond to celestial bodies, but in astrology, we work with nine planets and two celestial bodies in our solar system, yet there are only ten spheres on the Tree, so one planet or celestial body is going to get left out—or, in the mapping below, assigned to Da'ath, which is not really a sphere. We'll talk more about Da'ath in chapter 11. As the discovery of the outer planets of Uranus, Neptune, and Pluto is fairly recent compared to the bulk of the work that's been done on the Qabala, their correspondences on the Tree are a matter of some debate, and there's no universally agreed-upon placement for them yet. The correspondences I use for those planets are based on Ivo Dominguez Jr.'s *Practical Astrology for Witches and Pagans.*

Adding to the mathematical messiness of astrological correspondences to the spheres, the twenty-two paths in the Tree of Life correspond with three of the four elements (fire, water, air), seven of the celestial bodies (the moon, the sun, Mercury, Venus, Jupiter, Mars, and Saturn), and twelve astrological signs. There are good reasons for these alignments, but at first glance it does appear a bit random and haphazard. I'm not going to dive into the rationale for the correspondences in this book, but there are books in the further reading section on page 219 that do so, if you're interested in learning more.

Sphere or Path	Elemental or Astrological Correspondence
1: Kether	Neptune
2: Chokmah	Uranus
3: Binah	Saturn
Da'ath	Pluto
4: Chesed	Jupiter
5: Geburah	Mars

Sphere or Path	Elemental or Astrological Correspondence
6: Tiphareth	The Sun
7: Netzach	Venus
8: Hod	Mercury
9: Yesod	The Moon
10: Malkuth	Earth
11: Kether to Chokmah	Air
12: Kether to Binah	Mercury
13: Kether to Tiphareth	Moon
14: Chokmah to Binah	Venus
15: Chokmah to Tiphareth	Aries
16: Chokmah to Chesed	Taurus
17 Binah to Tiphareth	Gemini
18: Binah to Geburah	Cancer
19: Chesed to Geburah	Leo
20: Chesed to Tiphareth	Virgo
21: Chesed to Netzach	Jupiter
22: Geburah to Tiphareth	Libra
23: Geburah to Hod	Water
24: Tiphareth to Netzach	Scorpio
25: Tiphareth to Yesod	Sagittarius
26: Tiphareth to Hod	Capricorn
27: Netzach to Hod	Mars
28: Netzach to Yesod	Aquarius
29: Netzach to Malkuth	Pisces
30: Hod to Yesod	Sun
31: Hod to Malkuth	Fire
32: Yesod to Malkuth	Saturn

There are many ways you can use astrological correspondences in your work with Qabala.

When building an altar for a sphere, using the symbol of its corresponding celestial body can add power to your working.

When doing a working or meditation focused on a particular sphere, consider timing it to align with its planetary hour or appropriate day of the week for added power and synchronicity.

When looking at an astrological chart, consider the Qabala correspondences for the signs and planets and how they relate to the overall picture.

In the pathworkings in part 2, I'll include references to the corresponding celestial body for each sphere to build the connection between the two in your mind. In part 3, many of the workings will include planetary correspondences as well.

Now that you understand the basic components of the Tree of Life and its correspondences in tarot and astrology, let's take a tour of the spheres through a guided meditation.

GUIDED MEDITATION

Introduction to the Tree of Life

You may record this pathworking and play it back for yourself, have a friend read it, or read it and then walk through it based on your memory. I recommend keeping a journal and pen or other recording device nearby so you can write, draw, or record yourself speaking about your experience immediately after you complete the pathworking. Remember that you are in control of what happens here, and you may end up diverting course from what I've written. It's okay to do so!

Sit comfortably in a place where you will not be disturbed for the next fifteen minutes.

Take a deep breath in through your nose and out through your mouth. Take another deep breath, in and out. Close your eyes.

Feel your feet or your seat firm on the ground or on your chair. Feel the air entering your lungs. Feel the heat of the blood circulating in your body. Feel your heart beating. Bring yourself to a state of being present in this very moment. Now feel the passage of time, each second ticking by. Time limits us. Space limits us. But in time and space, we can create. We can take action. These are the blessings of Malkuth, the tenth sphere.

Fill your vision with the color purple. Now think of things that are purple. Picture them in your mind. What do you see? What do you smell? What do you taste? Are these things real? What is real? Here are the visions of everything that has ever been imagined, visions of what has been and what will be. This treasure house of images and possibilities is the blessing of the ninth sphere, Yesod, and also its curse, for its illusions can trick you.

Fill your vision with the color orange. Make that orange into the bookshelves of the grandest library you've ever seen. Everything known and everything sought to be understood is catalogued here, in Hod, the eighth sphere, where it is archived and named. As you walk around this library, you realize you are not alone, and in fact, several divine beings are also in this space, for this is the sphere where deities transform from pure energy into the shapes of lifeforms we can understand. Look at the floor, walls, and ceiling. You find them covered in scripts and symbols. This is where words and symbols are created, the containers of our magick that can bring wild energy into focus, and the ways in which we are able to communicate with each other.

Fill your vision with the color green. That green becomes the leaves of a dark forest. Smell and hear the abundance of life within a damp forest on a summer's day. Feel the humid, warm air on your skin and become aware of the heat of your own desire. Feel your blood pounding in your veins. Feel your will. It is the projective force of will and energy found here in Netzach, the seventh sphere, which, combined with the clarity and focus of Hod, creates magick.

Fill your vision with bright, gleaming gold. Now apply that color gold to the sphere within yourself that you identify as your center. Feel it drift within yourself until it finds a place where it feels perfectly balanced. Breathe and feel a deep sense of harmony within yourself and with the energies surrounding you in this room. You are here. You are centered. And here, on the center point of the Tree, in Tiphareth, the sixth sphere, is where that gleaming, shining point of equilibrium exists.

Fill your vision with a bright red. The red takes the shape of Superman's cape, then a flag on a battlefield, and then the gown of a judge as they deliver a just verdict. This is the sphere of justice, which allows the balance of Tiphareth to exist. When there is something in your life that no longer serves you, where there is excess, Geburah, the fifth sphere, seeks to rebalance the scale. Harsh but lasting lessons are learned here. Feel the fire of Geburah, red-hot and blazing, as it strikes you upon the anvil to shape you into the best version of you possible.

Fill your vision with royal blue. The blue becomes the water of a large map, showing a large plot of bare land. You find yourself staring at the map and then instinctively reaching for figures of buildings, walls, and bridges, placing them where they seem to fit best. While Geburah destroys and hones, Chesed, the fourth sphere, builds and envisions possibilities.

You feel the work you are doing is blessed—for it and you are part of the divine spark of creation, and by doing this act, your destiny and will are in perfect sync.

Fill your vision with deep, dark black. Smell the salty air and feel yourself rock gently on the waves as you sit on the deck of a ship. You cannot see, and you cannot hear the waves or any other sounds, but you have a profound sense of the vastness and extreme depth of the ocean that surrounds you. But even within the extreme depths of this roiling sea, even within that deep darkness and silence, there is life. Life is born. Life dies. The great mystery of that cycle is concealed here, in the darkness and silence of Binah, the third sphere.

Fill your vision with a brightly swirling, pearly gray. Feel your body caught in an effervescent tornado of energy, endlessly spinning and filling and bursting without end. You feel as though your every atom is dissipating and your aura expanding to fill an impossibly large space, spreading and rushing and going so very, very fast. In Chokmah, the second sphere, you no longer have form. You are part of a stream of pure, endless, rushing energy that fuels the universe, the never-ending expansion of the big bang.

Finally, feel yourself calm, and focus on a single tiny dot of pure, white brilliance. In this dot is everything. It is the ultimate place of unity. The entire plan of the universe, everything that ever was, is, or ever will be, every force and every ounce of energy, is contained within and originates from this bright, brilliant dot—Kether, the first sphere.

Now imagine the dot slowly fading away. Fill your vision with the swirling, pearly gray again ... and now deep, dark black ... and now royal blue ... bright red ... shining gold ... forest green ... orange ... purple ... and now become aware of the light of this room pressing on your eyelids. Take a deep breath. When you are ready, open your eyes.

If you have any thoughts or impressions from this pathworking you wish to remember, write or draw them in your journal, or record yourself speaking about them while they're still fresh in your mind.

Exercises to Deepen Your Understanding of the Tree

The Tree of Life isn't just something you learn about. It's something you need to engage with on a personal level. These exercises will help you connect the Tree to your life.

JOURNALING EXERCISE
Meditations on the Colors and Numbers

Each sphere has a color and a number associated with it. Spend some time meditating, then draw, freewrite, or record yourself speaking about what each color and number means to you. How do they feel? Do they have textures, temperature, or scents associated with them? Do you have particular spiritual associations with them?

Kether: 1: Brilliance, white, or clear

Chokmah: 2: Pearly gray

Binah: 3: Black

Chesed: 4: Royal blue

Geburah: 5: Bright red

Tiphareth: 6: Gold

Netzach: 7: Forest green

Hod: 8: Bright orange

Yesod: 9: Deep purple

Malkuth: 10: Citrine, olive, russet, and black

JOURNALING EXERCISE

What the Qabala Means to You Today

Whether you are new to working with Qabala or have been a practicing Qabalist for decades, take a moment to write down, draw, or record yourself speaking about your perceptions of the Tree of Life at this point in time. Keep getting thoughts out, without stopping, for five minutes. Set a timer! Don't worry about spelling, grammar, artistic value, or even if your thoughts make sense—just write, speak, or draw. When the time is up, finish your last thought, and then stop. Reread what you've written, listen to what you've recorded, or look at what you've drawn. Are there gleanings of new ways to look at the Tree of Life in there? Now put this work away and check it again when you've finished reading this book. You may be surprised by what you see.

Bringing It All Together

Qabala is a framework for understanding and exploring the universe and yourself based on a glyph called the Tree of Life. The Tree is a map of personal growth, a reminder that everything is divine, a filing cabinet for the universe, and a pathway into manifestation represented by the Lightning Flash. The Tree is basically one giant fractal, where every component contains and is contained by a larger whole, reminding us that patterns on the micro level are reflected on the macro level. Understanding the Tree can also help you understand other magickal systems and vice versa.

In the next chapter, we'll lay some groundwork on the concept of queer magick before we focus on Qabala as a queer magickal tool in chapter 3.

Queerness and Magick

Before we talk about the specifics of how Qabala is queer, let's look at queerness as a concept in magickal practice. The bad news is, many magickal communities and magickal practices have a fraught relationship with queer people and queer concepts. The good news is that by embracing a queer lens, we have the opportunity to not only make our communities more inclusive, but to deepen our personal practices and make them more powerful.

Magick Is Queer

Magick is inherently, intersectionally, gloriously queer: it's an anti-capitalist approach to claiming power that is open to people of all genders, sexualities, races, physical abilities, ages, and classes. In a magickal practice, we realize that true power lies not within hierarchical power structures but within ourselves, the planet, and the whole of the cosmos. Magickal practitioners work with spirits and beings that transcend any concept of gender, sometimes in a deeply intimate fashion that transcends any earthly concept of sexuality. Magick celebrates that which is liminal, that which lies beyond the conventional and easy-to-categorize-and-understand.

Our magickal communities tend to draw people from the fringes of society: those who have been rejected or don't fit into mainstream religion or culture. And yet, much of Pagan language, myth cycles, and symbol sets lionize cisheteronormativity, which is frankly alienating for queer people.[28] Examples of this include emphasizing myth cycles of a god and a goddess procreating, focusing magickal women's groups exclusively around menstruation and childbirth, and teaching people that magick happens when so-called *masculine* and *feminine* energy interact. If the way magick works is presented with symbols you don't relate to, or things your body simply cannot do, then it can be more challenging to develop an authentic magickal practice or feel comfortable within a magickal community. A place that is supposed to embrace us weirdos ends up only being safe and comfortable for those weirdos who still buy into cisheteronormative ideals.

If we want to grow our magickal communities and, more importantly, help empower people who have been disempowered by society, it's critical that we examine—in collaboration with people of various genders, races, heritages, physical abilities, ages, classes, sexualities, etc.—our language, our rituals, our symbols, and our belief structures. "We've always done it that way" is not a valid reason for alienating people and reinforcing harmful stereotypes.

We must work collaboratively to co-create spaces and structures that are welcoming and affirming, not ones that rely on outdated concepts that aren't reflective of this wonderful mosaic of a world. I'm glad to see many have taken up this work and are creating amazing, queer-inclusive communities and traditions, but there is always more work that can be done.

Queering Your Magickal Practice

In the introduction, I defined *to queer* as viewing something through a lens that calls into question anything we take for granted as *normal*. In

28. Magdalene, *Outside the Charmed Circle*, 7; Cassandra Snow, *Queering Your Craft: Witchcraft from the Margins* (Newburyport, MA: Weiser, 2020), xxi; Lee Harrington and Tai Fenix Kulystin, eds., *Queer Magic: Power Beyond Boundaries* (Anchorage: Mystic Productions Press, 2018), 2.

the academic discipline of queer theory, one breaks down and questions norms, roles, and traditional binaries, particularly those related to sex, sexuality, and gender.[29] But *queering* applies to things outside the realms of gender and sexuality too. Queering is intersectional in nature, including the subjects of race, class, disability, and more. The act of queering seeks to break down binaries, norms, and assumptions, often embracing the *both/ands* and *neither/nors*. Everyone's magickal practice can benefit from applying a queer lens. To queer your magickal practice is to add complexity and gray area, and to make your magick more reflective of the amazing diversity in our world.

One way you can queer your practice is to look at the language, rituals, deity relationships, and symbol sets you use and ask yourself: Why does this work for me? What assumptions am I making about myself, the world, and the way magick works by using these? What is true, and what is filtered through my own perception of the world? What is my perception of magickal power based on, and does that perception unwittingly disempower others? How can my approach to magick be more integrated, holistic, and empowering? Are there unnecessarily cisheteronormative concepts and binaries inherent within my work? The ideal outcome from this exercise isn't to cast your faith or practice into doubt, but rather to find ways to deepen and expand upon it, to make it more authentic to you and to the world in which you live.

Let's start by examining and breaking down a binary often found in magickal practice: the masculine/feminine energy binary, often referred to as *polarity*. The concept of polarity shows up in many magickal traditions and texts, including in Qabala study. In chapter 3, I'm going to show how the Tree of Life's energy flows are actually quite dynamic and nonbinary.

Polarity: Beyond the Binary

Polarity, in the context of magick, is the interaction between two opposing things to produce energy or encourage its flow. Let's talk a bit about

. . . .

29. Holleb, *The A–Z of Gender and Sexuality*, 214–16.

how binary concepts are used in magick and how we can expand upon this idea to be more queer-inclusive.

Some magickal traditions use the interplay of so-called *masculine* and *feminine* energies as the most basic form of raising energy in ritual and magick. The idea is that there is a type of energy that is projective and positive, and a type of energy that is receptive and negative, and by combining them, you get magick. This concept reminds me of furniture assembly instructions: "Insert tab A into slot B." The idea of a masculine/feminine energy binary, though problematic, can be useful as training wheels when you're first starting to learn magick because it's a metaphor most of us raised in a patriarchal society can understand pretty easily.

I'm not saying working with these two types of energy is ineffective, and I'm not saying those types of energy don't exist, but this approach is reductive, basic, and incomplete. It's also alienating to those of us who don't identify as masculine or feminine, or who don't identify with the cisheteronormative idea of masculine energy as projective and feminine energy as receptive. If we're going to categorize energy types, labeling some energies as *masculine* or *feminine* falls way short of what is possible. In fact:

It's overly simplistic and limiting from a magickal perspective. When you start to look into all the different energetic interaction patterns we use in other aspects of magickal practice—the elements, the pentacle, higher/middle/lower self, the zodiac, chakras, and, of course, the Qabala—you realize energy work is a lot more complicated than just two opposing points. The deeper I go into my practice, the less useful I find the concept of working with just two types of energy.

It reinforces harmful masculine and feminine stereotypes. Honestly, I would have less of a problem with the whole masculine/feminine energy binary concept if we didn't use those specific labels packaged with these definitions of what *masculine* and *feminine* mean:

Masculine energy is described as...	Feminine energy is described as...
Active	Passive
Projective	Receptive
Light	Dark
Positive (+)	Negative (–)

As someone assigned female at birth (AFAB), I am downright insulted that *feminine* is defined as *passive and receptive*. Not to put too fine a point on it, but this stereotype reinforces rape culture. The idea that masculinity means *taking action* while femininity means *receiving what is done to them* is a patriarchal relic best left in the gutter.

Using the language of *masculine* and *feminine* in magick can alienate nonbinary, agender, and genderqueer people. When you come into a magickal community, text, or ritual with your lived experience outside the gender binary and there's an attempt to indoctrinate you with traditional gender roles as a means of gaining or using magickal power, it's a slap in the face! We should immediately decouple the concept of binary, opposing types of energy from the concepts of *masculine* and *feminine* because keeping those concepts together is inaccurate, confusing, and harmful. What's more, there are alternatives. If you're wedded to this specific kind of binary interplay, instead of using *masculine/feminine* as shorthand, call these types of energy by their more descriptive terms, like *projective energy* and *receptive energy*.

There are also lots of binary but non-gender-based polarities you can use, and probably already are using, in magick. Some examples:

- Noise/silence (e.g., clapping or drumming)

- Inhaling/exhaling

- Right hands holding left hands in a circle

- Pushing/pulling

- Macrocosm/microcosm (as above, so below)

The Power of the Nonbinary and the Liminal

To move beyond binaries in your energy work, we've got a whole lexicon of symbols to choose from to explain different ways in which energy interacts, and many of us already use them in our magick. As I mentioned previously, we've got the elements, the pentacle, astrology, tarot, and, most relevant to this book, Qabala.

Working outside the binary is powerful. We can work with energies that resonate, energies that push against each other, energies that cycle and flow as a continuum, and energies that serve as different parts of a whole, like notes in a musical chord.[30]

If you're looking for some concrete ways to use nonbinary energy in magickal work, consider:

- Dance

- Music

- Resonance of "like" things

- Chanting

- Working with multiple elements

- Feeling the movement of planets passing through the signs

- Focusing on circulation and flow of energy

Another way to work beyond the binary is to incorporate liminal energy and experiences into our work. *Liminal* is the word used to describe the betwixt-and-between places or states of being, those that are neither one thing nor the other. A doorway, for example, is a liminal place: a spot between one room and another. The moments surrounding birth and death are liminal times in our existence, as we are moving between different states of being. States of trance and meditation put our minds into a liminal mode. Many believe that at certain times of year, the

. . . .

30. Yvonne Aburrow, "Inclusive Wicca Manifesto," in *Queer Magic: Power Beyond Boundaries*, ed. Lee Harrington and Tai Fenix Kulystin (Anchorage: Mystic Productions Press, 2018), 9–10; Ivo Dominguez, Jr., "Redefining and Repurposing Polarity," in *Queer Magic: Power Beyond Boundaries*, 177–78.

veils between the worlds are particularly thin, allowing us access to that liminal space between our world and the world of spirits and the ancestors. The Tree of Life has liminal veils separating the triangles. Embracing the liminal moments and spaces, things that are both-and-neither simultaneously, is already part of our spiritual vocabulary in magickal practice.

Take a moment to consider new ways you can draw upon the power of the liminal to deepen your work. For example:

- Bring mindful awareness to pauses and transitions in daily life: Pause to breathe as you move from one task to the next. Be fully conscious of your movements every time you change positions from lying down to sitting to standing.

- Consider doing magickal workings or meditations, where safe and possible, in outdoor liminal spaces: places where water and land meet, bridges, tunnels, clearings in the woods, or crossroads.

- Incorporate labyrinth walks into your practice, or buy, draw, or print a finger labyrinth to use as a meditation tool.

- Do magick with the waxing and waning moon; not just at the full and dark moons.

- Build intentional *margin time* into your life: unscheduled blocks you can use for rest, work, or magick as needed.

- Work with the paths in Qabala, traversing the liminal space between two archetypal concepts represented in the spheres.

- Experience the veils in Qabala that separate certain spheres from each other.

Working with nonbinary energy flows and working with liminal concepts are ways to apply a queer lens to your magickal practice: you're breaking down binaries and exploring that which does not fit neatly into a specific category. Adding this kind of depth and complexity to your magickal practice is powerful, and teaching a variety of ways in which energy moves, beyond a binary structure, makes it easier for queer people to see ourselves in our magickal tool sets and vocabularies.

In the next chapter, we'll begin exploring the complex energy patterns and liminal spaces in the Tree of Life.

JOURNALING EXERCISE
Nonbinary Energy Flows

Spend some time meditating, then record yourself speaking or write about the concepts of fire and water. In what ways are they similar? In what ways do they differ? More importantly, how do they interact? Water can douse fire, yes, but fire can also evaporate water and create steam. When we work with the elements of fire and water, what does that look like? Fire and water are not opposites, but they do have a specific relationship and different effects on each other, depending on the context. This is a perfect example of a polarity that isn't gender-related. Fire and water are two forces that can interact to create energy but are not set up in a masculine/projective vs. feminine/receptive way. Continue thinking about other elements and how they interact and see what you come up with!

Bringing It All Together

Magick is inherently queer, despite efforts to shoehorn it into a binary, cisheteronormative model. Queering your magickal practice is the opportunity to break down barriers, to examine deeply held assumptions, and use more inclusive symbol sets that better reflect the world around us. We can, for example, refresh the concept of polarity in magick: instead of using a masculine/feminine binary, we can look at non-gender-related binaries, liminal places, or nonbinary energy flows.

Now that we've laid the foundation of queer magick as a concept, let's turn our attention to the ways in which Qabala is a queer-inclusive magickal tool.

CHAPTER 3

Qabala Is Queer

In a world hell-bent on binaries, on emphasizing that everything must be *this* or *that* but never *both* or *neither,* the Tree of Life is refreshingly inclusive and fluid in its nature. Qabala embraces complexity, contradictions, gray area, and nuance.

Not only is the Tree of Life a symbol that encompasses all things that ever have been or ever will be, which includes all genders and sexualities, it is also a pictorial example of dynamic, complex, contradictory, and fluid metaphorical genders and sexualities. The Tree of Life is a symbol that reflects queer experiences and communities.

Though I believe the Tree is fundamentally queer, by calling attention to this aspect, I am engaging in the act of queering the Tree. In queering Qabala, we are closely examining and questioning that which is assumed as normal or default, particularly that which conforms to cisheteronormativity.

Why Bother Queering the Tree in the First Place?

Every generation of Qabalists has the duty to add to and deepen our understanding of the Tree of Life, and to that end, we need more Qabalists from a variety of life experiences and perspectives. As noted in the section on Qabala as a filing cabinet of the universe, all practitioners can add to that metaphorical filing cabinet. As in scientific fields, the discoveries, work, and documentation left by our forebears is, by its nature, incomplete. We have the opportunity to expand on that understanding and to contextualize it for today's magickal practitioners. Broadening the range of experiences Qabala practitioners bring to the table can only serve to improve and expand our collective knowledge and understanding of the Tree of Life. Qabala is and can be a tool that is egalitarian, inclusive, and empowering. By queering the Tree, we bring these facets to life and give potential queer Qabalists a more holistic perspective from which to do magickal work.

I want to emphasize that what I'm about to walk through are all aspects of the Tree and correspondences that already existed; none of this was added or twisted or otherwise rainbow-glittered by me. The Tree is queer by its very nature and structure, with the names and symbols already ascribed to it. It has aspects that are clearly agender, nonbinary, genderfluid, and bisexual.

Genderless Aspects of the Tree

To begin with, the Tree of Life is largely composed of archetypal concepts and experiences that transcend gender, both as a whole and as we look at its component parts. Starting above the topmost point of the Tree, we have the concepts of Ain (nothingness beyond our comprehension, the void), Ain Soph (infinite nothingness), and Ain Soph Aur (infinite light). These are the *veils of negative existence*, or, as famed occultist Lon Milo DuQuette calls them, "the three kinds of Nothing."[31] None of these concepts—void, infinity, infinite light—are gendered in their nature, and

....

31. Lon Milo DuQuette, *The Chicken Qabalah of Rabbi Lamed Ben Clifford: A Dilettante's Guide to What You Do and Do Not Need to Know to Become a Qabalist* (York Beach, ME: Weiser, 2001), 19.

they are the points of absolute infinity on the Tree. Note I do not say the points of absolute *divinity*, for the whole Tree is divine. We can also argue that none of the spheres or paths are gendered, as they comprise large, archetypal concepts and experiences. That, too, would be valid. Honestly, I could just say the Tree of Life transcends all concepts of gender and end the book right there. But that wouldn't be as fun as revealing how much these spheres play with the concept of gender, which I'll be doing throughout this book.

The Nonbinary Pillar

In the previous chapter, we broke down the masculine/feminine energy binary. Some traditions lean heavily on teaching this binary concept but rarely focus on that which lies between or apart from the masculine or feminine. As a nonbinary person, I was delighted to find my gender identity baked into the Tree.

You will notice the Tree of Life is full of groups of three: the three triangles and three pillars are echoes and reflections of the three veils of negative existence. As we discussed in the introduction to Qabala chapter, the Tree of Life has the Masculine Pillar (Pillar of Force, Pillar of Mercy), the Feminine Pillar (Pillar of Form, Pillar of Severity), and the Pillar of Balance in the middle—effectively, the Nonbinary Pillar.

The spheres on the Nonbinary Pillar include those of ultimate unity/potential (Kether), true balance and healing (Tiphareth), imagination (Yesod), and ultimate manifestation (Malkuth). Coincidentally, these spheres contain the colors of the nonbinary pride flag: Kether is white, Tiphareth is gold/yellow, Yesod is purple, and Malkuth contains black as one of its four colors. Arguably, Kether and Malkuth are particularly important spheres on the Tree, representing the beginning and the end of the path of manifestation. Tiphareth, between them, is the sphere assigned to the powers of the sun and healing, and marks the point of absolute balance on the Tree. Yesod, sitting below Tiphareth, is the sphere assigned to the moon, introspection, and imagination, and is both the last stop before birth and the first stop after death. In this way, the Tree of Life glyph acknowledges that the powers of unity and manifestation, balance, healing, imagination, birth, and death all transcend gender and binary polarity.

The spheres on the Pillars of Force and Form play a sort of energetic tug-of-war with each other until their energies meet in the Pillar of Balance. The four spheres on the Pillar of Balance unite, balance, and transform the forces from the spheres on either side of it, while adding their own energy to the mix. For example, Chesed is a sphere about expansion and vision, whereas Geburah is a sphere about destruction. Their energy flows into Tiphareth, the point of absolute balance on the Tree, where expansion and destruction work in harmony, becoming a healing, life-giving, balanced force. Similarly, Netzach is a sphere of wild, raw, passionate energy,

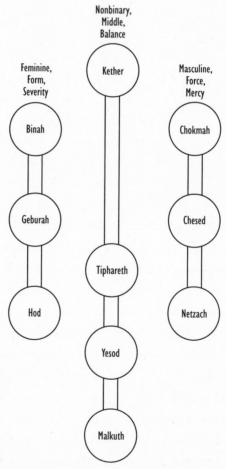

Figure 9: The three pillars on the Tree of Life

while Hod is a sphere of analysis, categorization, and forms. Their energy flows into Yesod, the sphere of the imagination and the sphere in which we do our magickal work. Magickal work needs a balance of raw energy and clear direction to be successful.

The Pillar of Balance is not described as a half-projective and half-restrictive force, but rather its own type of energy. In a similar way, many nonbinary people don't describe their gender as something existing in the middle of a spectrum between masculine and feminine: their gender exists on a separate axis entirely. The Pillar of Balance is an excellent representation of that separate axis, as its powers are unique and separate from those of the pillars alongside it, even as they unite and transmute the energies from those pillars.

I was lucky enough to experience this uniting, transmuting energy in my Second Degree ritual with the Assembly of the Sacred Wheel. In my tradition, the Second Degree ritual aims to unite the energies of force and form within yourself. Maybe not coincidentally, as this ritual's magick settled within me in the months following it, I realized and began to come to terms with my nonbinary gender identity: that third type of energy manifesting within me.

Genderfluid and Bisexual Aspects of the Tree

Do the spheres have genders? No. But also yes! Sort of. The Tree of Life plays really fast and loose with the concept of gender and the spheres.

Let's be frank: When we talk about the Tree of Life and its spheres, we're talking about very high-level archetypes that transcend human concepts of gender. However, humans named the spheres and pillars, and developed layers of metaphors and symbols to make the Tree easier to understand. The names and many of the metaphors have either implicit or explicit genders, and they are worth exploring, particularly because they are arranged in a super queer fashion. The people who added the pillar names, sphere names, magickal images, astrological correlations, and deity correlations were intriguingly inconsistent with gender alignment.

We know the pillars have a metaphorical gender—the Masculine Pillar, the Feminine Pillar, and what I'm calling the Nonbinary Pillar. One would think the Qabalists of old would put only masculine symbols on the Masculine Pillar, feminine symbols on the Feminine Pillar, and androgynous or ambiguous symbols on the Nonbinary Pillar.

But they absolutely did not.

Not only that, but within individual spheres, they used varying, contradictory symbol sets, some of which are explicitly queer, and the ways in which energy flows on the Tree are super queer as well.

Let's start by looking at energy flow on the Tree. When energy flows between spheres, you could view that as a metaphorical, heteronormative sexual act: One sphere is projecting energy, which is received by another

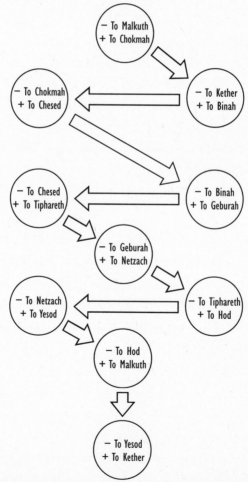

Figure 10: Polarities within spheres on the Lightning Flash

sphere. Or, to use an asexual metaphor, each sphere buds off to create the next sphere. Regardless of how you view it, each of the spheres sends energy in various directions on the Tree. Any place you see two spheres connected by a path, that represents an energy flow.

If you look at the energy pattern of the Lightning Flash—the flow of energy from Kether to Chokmah to Binah and so on down to Malkuth—you'll note that each sphere both sends energy to the spheres that follow them and receives energy from the spheres before them: demonstrating that each sphere is *both* projective *and* receptive. For example, Chokmah is projective to Binah while being receptive to Kether. In other words, Chokmah is genderfluid: acting in both the projective and receptive capacity, depending on the context. But it is also bisexual because it is interacting with Kether's masculine/projective aspect and Binah's feminine/receptive aspect.

The next area where the spheres' genders are a bit wibbly-wobbly lies in their names. Hebrew names have masculine or feminine endings, and that includes the names of the spheres.[32] As you look at the spheres' names, notice how the masculine names do not all align with the Masculine Pillar, nor do all the feminine names align with the Feminine Pillar. In fact, one of the three spheres on the Masculine Pillar has a feminine name, and one of the three spheres on the Feminine Pillar has a masculine name. While there is a rather satisfying gender parity among the ten spheres of the Tree—five of the spheres have masculine names and five have feminine names—they don't alternate masculine-feminine-masculine-feminine when you look at the Lightning Flash or the pillars.

You may also notice that Geburah and Chesed each have two names: one masculine and one feminine. Which name they're referred to depends on which book you're reading. Geburah and Chesed are the most common names you'll see for these spheres, but some texts may refer to Geburah (feminine) as Din (masculine), or Chesed (masculine) as Gedulah

· · · · · · · · · · · · · · · ·
32. Rachel Pollack, *The Kabbalah Tree: A Journey of Balance & Growth* (St. Paul, MN: Llewellyn Publications, 2004), 82–83.

(feminine). Given the fact that they have both masculine and feminine names, these spheres could rightly be considered genderfluid.

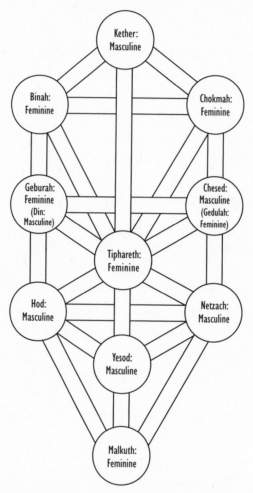

Figure 11: Masculine and feminine sphere names

We'll get into more detail on the individual spheres in part 2, but certain things are striking as we look at the sphere names here as related to the archetypes associated with them. For example, Chokmah and Binah, which are often said to represent the archetypal masculine and feminine, are both feminine names. The most commonly used name for the fifth sphere is Geburah, a feminine name, yet it is associated with Mars and destruction. Netzach, meanwhile, is a masculine name, yet is associated with symbols of feminine sexuality, particularly Venus. Tiphareth, the

sixth sphere, is a feminine name but is associated with the sun, including masculine sun deities like Apollo and Ra, as well as sacrificed kings.
Meanwhile, the moon, which in much magickal lore is strongly allied
with the feminine, is represented by Yesod: a sphere with a masculine
name. The inconsistencies between the Hebrew names, archetypes, and
magickal and astrological associations are hundreds of years old.

In the late 1800s, members of the Hermetic Order of the Golden
Dawn decided to add a new set of correspondences to the Tree: pictures
designed to represent each sphere and the energy it signifies. These are
called telesmatic images, telesmic images, or simply *magickal images.*[33]
These images are useful for meditation, helping you connect to the
spheres by anthropomorphizing them.

Sphere	Gender of Hebrew name	Pillar	Magickal image
Kether	Masculine	Nonbinary	Bearded ruler, in profile
Chokmah	Feminine	Masculine	Bearded man, facing forward
Binah	Feminine	Feminine	Mature woman
Chesed	Masculine	Masculine	Ruler on a throne
Geburah	Feminine	Feminine	Warrior in a chariot
Tiphareth	Feminine	Nonbinary	Sun child
Netzach	Masculine	Masculine	Beautiful naked woman
Hod	Masculine	Feminine	Person with a penis and breasts
Yesod	Masculine	Nonbinary	Very strong, naked man
Malkuth	Feminine	Nonbinary	Young queen, crowned and throned

Most of the images are gendered but do not align with either the gender
of the Hebrew names of the spheres or the pillars, though they do tend
to line up a bit better with the planetary deity correspondences: Netzach,
aligned with Venus, has the magickal image of a beautiful naked woman,
for example. And Geburah, aligned with Mars, has the magickal image of

. . . .

33. Reed, *The Witches Qabala*, 13.

a masculine warrior riding a chariot. There are notable exceptions to that alignment, however: Yesod—which, again, is most closely associated with the moon and its often-considered-feminine mysteries—has the magickal image of a strong, naked man.

And most intriguingly, the magickal image for Hod is that of a person with both a penis and breasts. We struggle to see intersex representation in pop culture today, yet intersex representation has been part of the Tree of Life for over one hundred years.

All this is to say: the metaphorical masculinity or femininity of a sphere is highly variable depending on whether you're looking at the sphere's name, the symbols and archetypes associated with it, or how its energy moves in relation to the spheres around it. And that … is incredibly queer.

Why Does This Matter?

If Qabala encompasses "life, the universe, and everything," then it encompasses queer identities regardless of the symbols and names on the Tree. But having the queerness be so explicit on the Tree—demonstrated with genderless archetypal concepts, a Nonbinary Pillar, universal bisexual energy flows, and spheres that represent multiple genders simultaneously—makes the Tree a particularly potent magickal tool for people with a more expansive view of gender and sexuality beyond the binary. It affirms that all genders and sexualities are both magickal and real. And it offers queer people a magickal tool to use in an authentic capacity as queer people: one that invites our whole personhood to the table. As we look at Qabala through a queer lens, Qabala can also become a lens itself to better understand queer life experiences.

Queering the Triangles

In chapter 1, we learned about the three triangles on the Tree of Life (Supernal, Ethical, and Astral) and how those represent different layers of consciousness or stages of evolution. When looking at the Tree from a queer perspective, I see these Triangles as representing distinct queer experiences. This is the beginning of me adding some rainbow sparkle and my own interpretation of aspects of the Tree of Life, which we'll continue in part 2.

Full caveats apply here: I am painting queer experiences with a fairly broad, archetypal brush. Every queer person is unique, so I can't claim everything in the chapters ahead is going to be authentic to or resonate with every queer person's experience. I'm going to focus on common threads and themes as best I can, based on my own experience within and research about the queer community. I encourage you to consider and adapt information about any of the queer experiences mentioned—discovering your own identity, coming out, and experiencing shared community—to your own personal context.

For many of us, our first experiences of being queer take place within our own minds and hearts, and eventually in the ways in which we express ourselves. It's a highly individual experience. Yesod, Hod, and

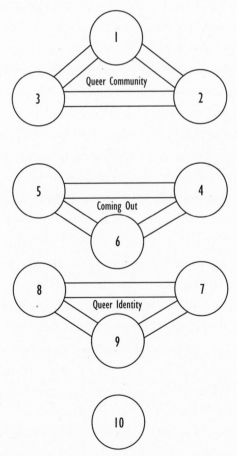

Figure 12: The triangles within the Tree of Life (queer)

Netzach—the Astral or Psychic Triangle—represent our personal identity and expression. This is the triangle closest to the manifest realm. Yesod is the sphere of the moon and imagination, where we can metaphorically try on different expressions of gender and sexuality. Hod is the sphere of categorization and naming, and is where we might consider our names, nicknames, and identity labels. Netzach is the sphere of sexuality and gender identity. I call this the Queer Identity Triangle.

The next part of the queer experience is the challenging growth experience of coming out. Tiphareth, Geburah, and Chesed, which comprise the Psychic Triangle, Mental Triangle, or Moral Triangle, express the coming-out process. In Tiphareth, the sphere of balance, is that moment when we come out to ourselves, realizing who we truly are and experiencing the peace that comes with that realization. In Geburah, we must let go of the pieces of ourselves that no longer fit, and in some cases, we must also let go of people in our lives who cannot handle our queer amazingness. In Chesed, we can plan and look to the future, imagining possibilities for ourselves and our identity. I call this the Coming Out Triangle.

After we come out, we find our community and unfold a fuller expression of ourselves, one that connects us to others. Binah, Chokmah, and Kether, which comprise the Supernal Triangle, represent experiences of queer community. In Binah, we grieve those who have been lost or hurt. In Chokmah, we experience the effusiveness of Pride. In Kether, we experience the joys of unity and solidarity. I call this the Queer Community Triangle.

These triangles provide a framework for understanding the individual spheres in a queer context by relating them to shared queer life experiences.

Bringing It All Together

The Tree of Life is a queer-inclusive magickal tool, having aspects that are clearly agender, nonbinary, genderfluid, asexual, and bisexual. Not only is there a Nonbinary Pillar between the Masculine and Feminine Pillars, but the symbol sets and names associated with the spheres have a lot of masculine/feminine symbol inconsistencies. The energy flow down the Lightning Flash involves every sphere acting in both a projective and receptive manner simultaneously, meaning the spheres are all metaphorically bisexual and genderfluid. Simultaneously, the entire Tree is composed of archetypal concepts that transcend the concept of gender or sexuality.

We've already put some rainbow glitter on the triangles, but we can go deeper in approaching the Tree of Life from a queer perspective. Let's now turn our attention to the spheres.

PART 2

The Spheres

E veryone teaching the spheres—also known as sephiroth—must make a choice: Start at Kether and work down to Malkuth, or start at Malkuth and work up to Kether? There is merit to either direction of study, but I find concepts easier to grasp when starting with the thing closest to my daily experience and building up to the most abstract things, rather than starting with the most abstract and working back to our consensus reality. So, I'm going to start at Malkuth and work up to Kether.

Each chapter in this section is devoted to one of the ten spheres, plus a chapter for the sphere-that-is-not-a-sphere, Da'ath. After an introduction to what the sphere is all about, one or more exercises to try, and an analysis of what makes that sphere queer and how to connect that sphere to queer experiences, there is a pathworking to help you get in touch with that sphere's energy. Note that the Da'ath chapter doesn't include a pathworking—I'll explain why when we get to that chapter. Please refer to "How to Use the Pathworkings in This Book" on page 11 for guidance on how best to make use of the pathworkings.

Malkuth: Super Queer Queen of Everything

We begin our journey in Malkuth. To understand the realms beyond physical existence, we must first understand our own plane. The patterns we experience in this realm of manifestation reflect throughout the Tree of Life.

Malkuth is the tenth sphere, depicted at the bottom of the Tree of Life, and represents the powers of manifestation. The name Malkuth means *Kingdom*, and it is everything that ever was, is, and will be on this physical plane: the whole universe.

It's not just tangible stuff, though. Malkuth also includes the subtle, psychic aspect of matter (auras, the elemental concepts of earth, air, fire, and water, etc.) as well as the overworld and underworld. The overworld and underworld include those who have previously had physical existence (ancestors) or have an analogue in physical existence (the Fae, nature spirits).

Many mainstream religions teach that the earth plane is evil and we must elevate our consciousness beyond it as soon as possible. Unfortunately, focusing on *transcendence* at the expense of *existence* hurts both our ability to function on this plane and our spiritual evolution. If you've been around magickal practitioners for any length of time, you've probably met people who can't manage their personal lives at all but claim to have a deep connection with other realms. These people need to learn how to ground themselves and remember that their work is based on this plane. While contact with other realms can help us spiritually develop, our spiritual work and growth happen here, in our incarnated state, on this plane.

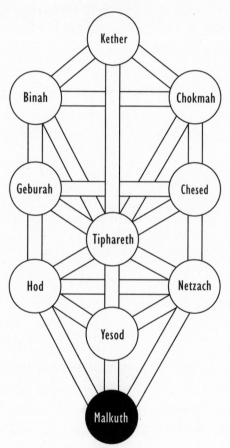

Figure 13: Malkuth

That said, we don't need to go beyond manifest reality to find divinity, as all spheres are divine, including Malkuth. Divinity is in everything, from trees to rocks to people to amoebas. Those of us who are animists believe that everything has a soul, including seemingly inanimate objects. But even those who aren't animists can experience profound beauty looking at a mountain, be in awe of the depth and vastness of the ocean, and wonder at the strength of the wind. Malkuth is divine because everything is divine.

Malkuth is also the tangible reflection of Kether, the most unmanifest of spheres. Kether represents pure potential. It contains the blueprint for all things. That which is possible in Kether may be made manifest in Malkuth. So even those who revere Kether as the most pure and holy of spheres must admit that Malkuth is its twin, and therefore equally divine.

Qabalists like to say, "Malkuth is in Kether, and Kether is in Malkuth." This describes the relationship between the two spheres in a few different ways. Firstly, Malkuth is the manifestation of the potential in Kether. In the physical, there is the spark of the eternal. In the eternal, there is the potential for the physical. We see this relationship as a partnership of two equal rulers described in the magickal images of these two spheres: Kether is seen as a bearded ruler, viewed in profile, and Malkuth is portrayed as a young queen, crowned and throned. Secondly, as discussed in the section on the four worlds, every sphere contains its own Tree of Life, so there literally is a Kether in Malkuth and a Malkuth in Kether (and a Geburah, a Chesed, etc.). Thirdly, as we looked at in the section on the four worlds, the Kether of one world's Tree can be seen as the Malkuth of the next world's Tree. Finally, and most paradoxically, the Tree of Life glyph is imperfect, and the Tree actually resembles more of a spiral that folds in upon itself, where Kether is overlaid upon Malkuth in a Möbius strip sort of way. You can cast a ritual circle that works with this idea, with both Kether and Malkuth in the north, and the other spheres from the Middle Pillar, including Da'ath, in the other three directions.[34]

Malkuth is referred to as the *Gate of Death*. The path that connects Malkuth to Yesod is the one we travel when we're born and when we die: when our spirits manifest on this plane and when they leave, in other

....

34. Ivo Dominguez Jr., *Keys to Perception: A Practical Guide to Psychic Development* (York Beach, ME: Weiser, 2017), 105.

words. "Why not call it the Gate of Birth *and* Death?" you might ask. Birth and death are one and the same, though our experiences of them as living beings may seem different. Birth, in a way, is a different experience of death. When we're born, when our spirits manifest in these physical bodies, we lose at least some of our awareness of our connection with the eternal. We are no longer potential: we are manifested, which gives us both incredible power and incredible limitations. And when we die, of course, we lose our physical existence on this plane, which gives us different, but still incredible, power and limitations.

The plane in which we exist is divine, necessary, and important. Unfortunately, some people miss this lesson and use magick as a way to escape this reality. They want to ignore this world and focus on those that lie beyond. This is no way to live! If I were to sum up the key lesson of Malkuth for magickal practitioners, it would be: "We live here. So *live. Here.*" Enjoy your time here, manifested, on this planet, where you can eat ripe peaches and breathe fresh air and talk to interesting people and listen to music and dance! A tree can't grow without a strong root structure, and Malkuth is where you have to cultivate those roots if you want to reach skyward.

So how do you cultivate those roots? Daily magickal practice is a big part of it. Daily meditation, breathing, and grounding and centering exercises help immensely in keeping us rooted yet also open to the forces beyond this plane. Shielding work is also critical, especially for those of us with strong empathic abilities. Being able to separate what is *you* and what is *not you* makes the experience of being embodied easier.

Daily magickal practice is one facet of the overall concept of self-care, which is the linchpin for all effective magickal work. Our spiritual work runs on the engine of our bodies and our minds, and therefore our magick is so much more effective and powerful when our bodies and minds are nourished and cared for. It may not seem like magick in and of itself, but getting enough rest, eating nutritious food, exercising in ways you find pleasurable, and getting professional psychiatric and medical attention when needed can only help you in rooting to this plane and being able to work magick. Caring for ourselves makes it easier to be conscious of and comfortable with embodiment. It can keep our consciousness focused on this plane and in this moment in time.

But being rooted also comes with the risk of becoming *stuck*. Inertia is the biggest risk of working in Malkuth without also reaching into the other spheres. Malkuth's energy can sometimes feel heavy, lodestone-like, and tired: this is part of why people sometimes yearn to escape and raise their consciousness higher on the Tree of Life before they've fully established their roots. Malkuth, after all, ages us. Working with Yesod keeps us young. More on that in the next chapter.

EXERCISE
Grounding, Centering, and Shielding

It's important to ground, center, and shield yourself each day, particularly before any magickal work. Here's one of many easy methods:

Stand if you are able, but you can also do this exercise seated or even reclined. Take three deep breaths, slowly. With each exhalation, let go of any tension you find in your body, almost as if you were slipping off a backpack full of worries. Don't worry; you can pick it up later.

Next, close your eyes. Become aware of your feet, firm on the ground, or whatever point of your body is most closely connected with the surface you're on. On your next exhale, imagine roots growing down from that point. Continue pushing your roots down, through the floor, through the foundation, down through the bedrock, deep, deep down into the earth.

Keep reaching those roots down until you feel warmth. You may feel it pulsing. If you don't, that's okay. You may experience this more visually or audibly than physically; everyone's magickal senses are different.

On your next inhale, draw that deep earth energy up through your roots and keep drawing it up, like you're sipping through a straw. Draw it up until you feel it touching your physical form, then keep drawing it up through your whole body, part by part. Imagine that warmth spilling out your head and down onto the ground.

On your next exhale, keep that feeling of warmth within you, and imagine branches growing out of the top of your head. Feel them reach up, and up, and up—through the ceiling, through the roof, up into the stratosphere, and out into space. Keep reaching those branches up until you feel a sort of crystalline or effervescent coolness. You may experience this more visually or audibly than physically; everyone's magickal senses are different. Draw that energy downward, down through the stratosphere, down through the roof, through the ceiling, and back into you.

Feel the energy above mixing with the energy from below. Feel the earth energy moving up and the cosmos energy moving down through you. Take another deep breath.

Now, place your hands out in front of you, palms facing outward, like you're pushing on a wall. On your next exhale, imagine the energy you're connected to above and below flowing through you and out of the palms of your hands, forming a bright mist that completely surrounds you. On your next exhale, imagine that mist forming a semipermeable bubble or net of energy around you. Tell it, out loud if you wish, to protect you from unwanted energy and anything else you'd like to be protected from, while allowing you to drain off excess energy—that's why the semipermeable part is important.

Finally, visualize that bubble or net around you taking on a chaotic black, white, and gray pattern, like static. This is an added layer to your shield, to hide you when needed.

When you're done, say, with confidence and full belief in yourself, "I am protected." If you wish, add, "So mote it be," "And so it is," or whatever wording seems natural to you in your practice.

Do this practice every day and before any magickal working.

What Makes Malkuth Queer?

Malkuth sits at the base of the Pillar of Balance, or what I'm calling the Nonbinary Pillar, that stands between the Masculine and Feminine Pillars on the tree. The concept of manifestation is a unification of the powers of force and form, creating that third kind of transmuted energy we noted in the section on the Nonbinary Pillar.

As the representation of all that is manifest, Malkuth is both omnigender and omnisexual because it represents all things and all beings that have existed, do exist, and will exist, including all genders and sexualities.

Malkuth is separate and unique in terms of the Tree of Life: it's the only sphere devoted specifically to manifest reality and sits apart from the three triangles in the Tree. Much like every queer story is unique and often includes themes of feeling alienated from mainstream culture, Malkuth is its own thing: part of, yet separate from, the rest of the Tree of Life.

And it's colorful too! Sitting beneath the gorgeous pride rainbow of the spheres above it, Malkuth is the only sphere with multiple colors assigned to it (citrine, russet, olive, and black). Malkuth just can't help letting that freak flag fly!

Why does Malkuth have four colors? You can think of them as representing the overworld, the underworld, the here and now, and that which is betwixt and between (the Fae realms, for example). They also represent the four elements (earth, air, fire, and water) at their lowest vibration closest to this plane.

It may seem silly to have a pathworking to experience Malkuth—after all, we live here! But our minds are often *not* in the here and now. We worry about the future, overthink things we've said or done, daydream … our thoughts rarely stay in the present moment. So, I encourage you to do the following pathworking.

Pathworking to Experience Malkuth

You may record this pathworking and play it back for yourself, have a friend read it, or read it and then walk through it based on your memory. I recommend keeping a journal and pen or recording device nearby so you can write about, draw, or record yourself speaking about your experience immediately after you complete the pathworking. Remember that you are in control of what happens here, and you may end up diverting course from what I've written. It's okay to do so!

Sit comfortably in a place where you will not be disturbed for the next fifteen minutes.

Close your eyes. Take three deep breaths, slowly, in and out. With each exhalation, let go of any tension you find in your body.

Without opening your eyes, visualize the room around you. Now picture it filling with a gray mist, starting at the floor and working its way up to the ceiling until the only thing you can see is grayness. As the mist dissipates, you find yourself standing in a grassy field with a gray, roiling sky above you, heralding a storm to come.

You feel the wind in your face, and the air tastes faintly of metal. You watch the tall grasses around you whip back and forth in the wind. In the distance, you see a forest with a path leading into it. You decide to seek shelter before the storm arrives and set off through the field toward the path. Thunder begins to rumble in the distance as you enter the woods.

You follow the path, listening to the anxious buzzing of insects and the thunder getting louder as you walk purposefully onward in hopes of finding some kind of cave or other shelter before the rain starts. The trees begin to get denser, and your path gets darker. And then you see something strange—branches bent into an archway over the path just ahead, and beyond the archway, there is … pure darkness. You feel uneasy but decide to press on, and when you get to the archway, you hear a friendly, youthful voice bidding you to come inside.

You take a deep breath and step through the archway, and are surprised to feel warmth and see sunlight streaming through windows on the other side as you step into a comfortable but small throne room made of gray stone. You smell roses in vases all around you and see a warm fire burning in the hearth on the wall to your left. There are several children sitting on fluffy cushions colored russet, olive, citrine, and black around the stone floor, playing games with blocks and cards. Then you see a modest throne made of rough branches covered in thick blankets and cushions in the middle of the wall opposite you. Nobody is sitting on the throne, however, and you look around to see if you can find who called to you from the archway.

"Hi," says the bright voice of a young adult to your right, and you turn to see a grinning, fresh-faced twentysomething richly attired in russet, citrine, olive, and black velvet, wearing a modest crown made of twigs shaped into little X's. Their bright eyes are friendly and kind. They welcome you to their throne room and thank you for visiting as they bow to you. You return the greeting and thank them for their hospitality. They reach for a tray heaped with brightly colored fruit and offer you some. You pick up a piece of fruit and take a bite, closing your eyes briefly as its juices burst in your mouth. It is the sweetest, most perfect fruit you've ever tasted. You finish eating it, wiping a bit of errant fruit juice from your chin bashfully as your host just smiles and offers you a bowl of warm water and a towel to clean the fruit juices off your hands, then leads you through the maze of children to a heavy wooden door to the right.

The next room is much larger and has a giant rug featuring the Tree of Life glyph. More children are in this room playing some complex game sort of like tag as they skip along the paths of the glyph on the rug in various directions and cheer when someone reaches Malkuth. Your host smiles and explains the children are playing a game called "Manifest." They explain the goal is to make it from Kether to Malkuth, passing through all the other spheres on the way so they can be manifested into the physical realm.

Your host then takes your hand and looks into your eyes. "You have been given a gift," they say. "The gift of living on the physical plane. You have the opportunity to do and learn so many things. Tell me, what kinds of things do you love to do, and what are you learning right now?" Answer them.

(Pause.)

Your host then asks, "How do you experience the beauty of the physical world? How do you keep your eyes open to the wonders that surround you even during difficult times?" Answer them.

(Pause.)

Your host then asks, "How do you keep yourself from becoming overwhelmed by responsibility and focus on the things that matter most?" Answer them.

(Pause.)

Your host thanks you and asks you to continue thinking about your answers in the days ahead. They encourage you to remember to be present in the moment as often as you can, to fully taste your food, deeply smell the flowers, truly feel the textures you encounter, and give yourself gratitude for the things your body allows you to do.

"Remember, divinity is within everything," they say as they lead you back into the throne room and return you to the archway. You can see nothing but darkness on the other side, but this time, you are not afraid of what you may encounter when you step through. You thank your host and bid them farewell, and they smile and bow in kind. You turn to step through the archway and are surprised to find that you are back on the path in the woods, but sunlight is streaming through the leaves and there's no hint of storm in the sky.

As you walk along the path, you notice all the different sounds of various bugs and birds and animals scurrying around, and smell an array of flowers and greenery around you. You admire the way the sunlight dapples your path and glints upon the wing of a bird that soars beneath the trees. You reach down to touch the wild clover growing alongside the path, noting how soft and smooth the leaves feel.

Eventually, you return to the field, and instead of a strong wind, you feel a gentle breeze and sunlight on your skin, and smell the loamy earth and grass. You breathe deeply, feeling the air fill your lungs. Eventually, the air around you fills with a pearly gray mist until you can no longer see the field. When the mist dissipates, you find yourself seated comfortably once more. Take a deep breath, wiggle your fingers and your toes, and when you are ready, open your eyes.

If you have any thoughts or impressions from this pathworking you wish to remember, write or draw them in your journal, or record yourself speaking about them while they're still fresh in your mind.

Bringing It All Together

The joys of Malkuth are about being present and appreciating all that is here on this plane of existence. By grounding our magickal work in the here and now, and by practicing mindfulness, we put down roots that keep us stable as we journey up the Tree of Life. Malkuth invites us to celebrate the glorious diversity of all that which is and has been manifested, including all the genders and sexualities here on Earth. In the chapters ahead, we will leave the manifested realm and journey into progressively less tangible and more archetypal spheres, starting with the sphere of imagination, Yesod.

Yesod: The Ultimate Drag Queen

Yesod is the ninth sphere on the Tree of Life, sitting directly above Malkuth. It synthetizes the powers that flow from the eight spheres above it into a digestible form for manifestation. Its name means *Foundation*. It makes reality possible and is the final editor of all possibilities before they get to our plane. As such, there are a lot of *impossible* and *untrue* things in Yesod, which is why it's the sphere of illusion.

As the Treasurehouse of Images that holds both the real and the imaginary, Yesod makes it easy to get caught up in illusions and believe them to be real, or to believe you have all the answers because you've made contact with something that *feels* true, much like when you wake from a particularly vivid dream. This is the danger of Yesod. One example of this is when someone early in their mystical journey suddenly believes they have come into contact with the ultimate truth and have all the answers. (They don't.) Teasing apart the real and the illusory in spiritual truths takes time, discernment, and maturity.

Illusions, however, are important. Imagination is important. And while it may initially seem counterintuitive that illusions and imagination, both ephemeral things, are held within the sphere that means *Foundation*, Yesod's role in our lives and in our reality is critical. As the old adage goes, "Change or die." Yesod can take us from understanding what things *are* to what things *could be*. Without imagination, there is no progress, no development, no evolution, because we lose our ability to adapt to change or envision improvements in our world.

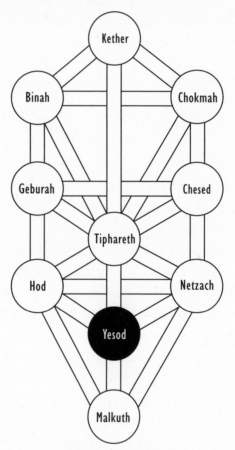

Figure 14: Yesod

Further, to be a magickal practitioner, you need an excellent imagination because you must visualize that which you are trying to create so vividly that you can believe it is real. You must infuse your idea with both energy and structure. In short, Yesod is where magickal practitioners do our magick. Yesod is the foundation because it's where you'll find energetic patterns that support manifestation.

By using our imaginations and considering what could be and how to make it so, Yesod allows us to move beyond our perceived physical, mental, and emotional limitations. Yesod helps us grow. It is a foundation, but a flexible foundation. If you stay active in Yesod, working with and cultivating your imagination, you don't become brittle, bitter, and stubborn. Yesod is vital, particularly as you age, when it can be tempting to let go of your imagination and dreams, to become so set on what you believe to be true and what you like and don't like, that you stop trying new things or considering new possibilities. Those who do not reach for the powers of Yesod can become convinced of their rightness in all things and close their minds to alternate viewpoints and possibilities.

Depending on which way you're traveling, either down or up the Tree, Yesod is either the last stop before manifestation or the first stop after a soul departs Malkuth. According to the laws of physics, matter cannot be created or destroyed; instead, matter becomes energy and vice versa. When you move between Yesod and Malkuth, regardless of direction, you experience integration. In one direction, we are integrating with physical form; in another, with the larger cosmos. This point of transformation between Malkuth and Yesod is one of the veils found in the Tree of Life. In this book's pathworkings where we travel up the Middle Pillar, this veil is represented in the pathworkings as a dark ring in the sky.

As we consider that our experience of death leads to Yesod as the sphere of illusion, it makes sense that there is diversity in near-death experiences. People will see what they expect to see. Does that make one person's interpretation correct and another's incorrect? No. They are simply experiencing Yesod from their own perspective. They are creating their reality in that moment.

In a way, Yesod is the soul of manifested reality. Yesod is our collective consciousness and collective unconsciousness, the vast web of connection between everything in this reality. This is referred to as the Machinery of the Universe: the connections between the planets, deities, plants, animals, bacteria, people—everything. We use the term *machinery* because each piece affects all the other pieces, like thousands of cogs turning each other in a giant contraption. We are all connected. We are all one. It's hard to perceive these connections most of the time, but if you are lucky enough to glimpse the vision of it all, it is breathtaking and instructive. As magickal practitioners, we seek to find and move along these gears, to move with and subtly shift the energies of the universe, to create ripples in the fabric of space and time that align us with the greatest good for ourselves and others. We begin to see and trust the subtle patterns of things on the micro level that reflect patterns on the macro level. We understand we have a role to play and that we, and everyone around us, are important.

∾

EXERCISE
Visualizing an Apple

In this exercise, we'll practice visualization, noting specific details of all the senses to strengthen the imaginative powers of Yesod within ourselves. If you find this exercise difficult, try it right after examining, holding, and biting into an apple. It's okay if you'd prefer to use another fruit or food as your focus, and it's also okay if you find one sense easier to call to mind than the others. Just keep practicing.

Close your eyes. Center yourself by breathing deeply and slowly. Become conscious of the sensations and sounds around you. I recommend doing the grounding exercise from the Malkuth chapter.

Now imagine an apple with as much detail as you can. Start with how it looks. What color is the skin? Does it have a stem? Does that stem have a leaf? Is it still attached to a tree? Are there bruises or maybe a hole where an insect has eaten away at it a little?

Hold the image in your mind while imagining what that apple feels like in your hand. How much does it weigh? What is the texture of the skin? Of the stem? How about that little rough spot on the opposite side of the stem? Is the skin perfectly smooth, or are there rough spots or irregularities?

Hold the vision and sensation of the apple in your mind while imagining what it feels like to bite into the apple. How does it feel against your teeth? Your tongue? What does it taste like? Is it juicy or dry? Is it soft or crisp? Is it tart or sweet? What is the sound of biting into it? Can you feel juice running onto your hand? Can you smell the apple? Now imagine chewing and then swallowing the apple. What does that feel like? Can you feel the apple sliding down your throat? Do you have any skin stuck between your teeth?

After you've spent a few minutes on this visualization, take a deep breath, clear your mind, and open your eyes.

EXERCISE
Scrying

Scrying is a type of divination that involves gazing into a substance, surface, or reflection. In this exercise, we'll scry into a flame and its reflection in a mirror to tap into the Yesod powers of connection within ourselves.

Materials:

- A tea light (small candle)

- A match or lighter

- A small mirror

- A quiet space where you can turn out the lights for a while

Setup:

Lay the mirror flat and place the candle on its surface. Light the candle. Turn out the lights and find a comfortable seated position next to the candle.

The Work:

Breathe deep. Do the grounding exercise from the Malkuth chapter. When you feel centered and present, gaze at the candle and its reflection on the mirror. Let your vision relax. Breathe. Watch the shapes and patterns that appear on the mirror and in the flame. Keep your mind clear. What do you see? Do any messages pop into your mind? Pay attention to them. If you get distracted, don't worry—just breathe and focus on the candle again.

It's okay if you don't see anything. Keep practicing, and something will come eventually.

What Makes Yesod Queer?

You can think of Yesod, the Treasurehouse of Images, as the universe's clothes closet with infinite possibilities. Yesod turns truths to illusions and illusions to truths, just like drag artists do. The art of drag is all about illusion: using makeup and clothing to imitate and exaggerate stereotypical gender signifiers for entertainment, often while lip-syncing. Drag, like Yesod, begs the question, "What *is* reality, anyway?"

Beyond the art of drag, though, using our imagination to play with different looks and personae is one of the key parts of a queer discovery journey. Yesod is part of the Queer Identity Triangle—the triangle made up of spheres that help define who you are. When you suddenly find yourself outside the norm of society, you realize the rulebook you've been taught no longer applies, and you need to try some new things on to see what fits. It's both exciting and terrifying. There are so many possibilities! What is your style, not just in clothing and accessories, but in hair, makeup, tattoos, or piercings? What about the kind of slang you use or how you spend your time in community? What feels right to you? Sometimes this process of imagining and trying and testing things takes years, and that's okay! Sometimes we try something for a while and decide we don't like it, so we try something else. That's okay too! It's totally natural for styles and taste and what we consider *fun* to shift and change over time. That's the joy of the illusions of Yesod: nothing is permanent, and the possibilities are endless.

This process of trying on personae isn't unique to the queer community, but it is definitely one of the rites of passage of being queer, and queer people tend to approach this process in a more genuine way than mainstream society. Mainstream society pays lip service to the idea of *finding yourself* and *being yourself,* but may only offer acceptance for a version of self that fits neatly in a particular box within your culture. There are exceptions to this, of course, but generally speaking, within the queer community, we celebrate people being proudly themselves, in whatever form that takes. Weird is good! Outrageous is good! Quiet and introspective is good too!

I had a glorious moment of celebrating someone expressing their unique identity when I was with my band, the Misbehavin' Maidens, at a sci-fi/fantasy convention in January of 2020. A group of queer teens walked up to our booth, and when they saw our many pride flag buttons, they proceeded to squee at the selection and carefully select what to buy. One of the teens proudly announced to me, in the course of conversation, that their gender identity was *alien.* And that moment gave me such hope for the future, particularly as a nonbinary person. It was a joy to behold this person's confidence and pleasure with the unique self they were discovering and becoming comfortable with at an age much younger than I was when I began to realize my own gender identity. The kids are all right.

It's fitting that Yesod, the sphere of the imagination, sits on the Nonbinary Pillar and is very inconsistent from a gender symbol set perspective. It is associated with the moon, a symbol frequently ascribed to the feminine, and yet its magickal image is that of a very strong, naked man, and its Hebrew name is masculine. It's a unification point of that which is considered force, form, and balance—or, put another way, masculine, feminine, and nonbinary energies.

Yesod is the point on the Tree of Life where all three pillars meet and bring their energy together before it becomes manifested, and there's something incredibly potent about that. Before something can become real, it has to come from this lovely energetic cocktail that's a mix of everything from the spheres above: masculine, feminine, both, and neither; passionate, analytical, balanced, mercenary, visionary, containerized, expansive, and pure potential. All of that blends into the visionary world of Yesod. Mixing lots of different kinds of energies and gender concepts together in the sphere of imagination makes Yesod super queer.

Pathworking to Experience Yesod

You may record this pathworking and play it back for yourself, have a friend read it, or read it and then walk through it based on your memory. I recommend keeping a journal and pen or recording device nearby so you can write about, draw, or record yourself speaking about your experience immediately after you complete the pathworking. Remember that you are in control of what happens here, and you may end up diverting course from what I've written. It's okay to do so!

Sit comfortably in a place where you will not be disturbed for the next fifteen minutes.

Close your eyes. Take three deep breaths, slowly, in and out. With each exhalation, let go of any tension you find in your body.

Without opening your eyes, visualize the room around you. Now picture it filling with a gray mist, starting at the floor and working its way up to the ceiling until the only thing you can see is grayness. As the mist dissipates, you find yourself sitting on a small wooden platform in a grassy field on a warm summer night. You hear crickets and other insects chirping and smell damp greenery all around. Looking up, you see it's a clear night with a beautiful full moon.

Looking down, you see the platform is a wooden circle about a meter in width. The circle is divided into quadrants painted olive, russet, citrine, and black. As you examine it, you realize it's floating a few inches above the ground. And then it begins to rise higher. The field and its sounds and smells fade into the distance as you rise higher into the atmosphere. You can breathe normally and are unafraid of the height—the platform feels stable and secure.

You look up and notice there is a large, dark ring hanging in the air. You pass through it and suddenly the moon is much larger in the sky, much closer to you, as if you've just jumped tens of thousands of miles in an instant. The moon gets larger and larger and you feel yourself drawn to it, yearning to be on its surface. You can feel its pull upon the ocean tides, the ebb and flow of its energy, and you desire to be part of that energetic flow, to ride the waves.

Suddenly, a purple mist surrounds you, obscuring your view of the moon, and when it dissipates the platform and the moon have vanished, and you find yourself in a vast clothes closet, crammed full of every possible style of every possible article of clothing you could imagine.

A friendly voice greets you, and you look over the racks in front of you to see a very muscular, naked person smiling kindly at you. They have an illuminated crescent moon shape on their forehead but are otherwise unadorned. "Welcome to the Treasurehouse of Images," they say. "If my nakedness makes you uncomfortable, simply imagine whatever clothes you wish and I will wear them for you."

(Pause.)

They lead you around the massive closet, and you begin to realize it isn't a closet at all but a veritable mansion full of nothing but clothes, shoes, and accessories. And the selection is constantly shifting and changing! What seems to be a rack full of red formal gowns one second becomes a showcase of avant-garde neckties the next. A pile of top hats in various sizes and colors morphs into a display case of sparkly heels. It's dizzying and overwhelming and tempting in equal measure. You can feel the shifts within you, rolling like tides all around you, an undulating rhythm you can feel deep inside, a feeling of desire.

Your host leads you to a wall-sized mirror, and you look at your reflection. They bid you to see yourself truly. What do you notice? What do you see?

(Pause.)

Your host asks you to look at what you want to become, and you gasp as your image shifts. What do you look like now?

(Pause.)

Your image in the mirror vanishes and is replaced with a collection of various objects and symbols. Your host explains that these are all tools that can help you grow and develop into the person you want to become, but you cannot use them all at once. Examine the items shown in the mirror.

(Pause.)

Choose one or two of the objects to take with you and examine them closely.

(Pause.)

Your host may have something to say about your choices: listen.

(Pause.)

When you've finished talking, your host guides you to an elevator. You notice the floor of the elevator is the wooden platform you took to get here. They bid you farewell, and you thank them for their guidance. You get into the elevator and the doors close. The night sky surrounds you. You think on your gifts as you zoom back through space, the moon appearing once more and growing smaller and smaller, then jumping to much smaller when you pass through the dark ring once again. You make a soft landing back on the field where you started and hear the insects buzzing all around you. You gaze at the moon one last time, whispering a thanks for the experiences you've had.

Eventually, the air around you fills with a pearly gray mist until you can no longer see the field. When the mist dissipates, you find yourself seated comfortably once more. Take a deep breath, wiggle your fingers and your toes, and when you are ready, open your eyes. If you have any thoughts or impressions from this pathworking you wish to remember, write or draw them in your journal, or record yourself speaking about them while they're still fresh in your mind.

Bringing It All Together

Yesod is ripe with possibilities and ideas we can try on as we develop our queer identities. Building a flexible foundation for the rest of the Tree of Life upon the kingdom of manifested reality, Yesod allows us to open our minds and our imaginations, hone our visualization and introspection skills, and use those abilities to ascend the Tree. It is also the mixing bowl and editor of all the energies from the spheres above before they become manifested in Malkuth. Everything that finds its way into Yesod gets its name from Hod, the next sphere.

CHAPTER 6

Hod: Analytical, Ace, Intersex

Hod is the eighth sphere on the tree and the lowest sphere on the Feminine Pillar, also known as the Pillar of Form or Pillar of Severity. Its name means *Glory*, and it's part of the lowest pair of spheres on the tree, sitting across from Netzach. Hod has a critical role to play in our understanding of the world around us, in our magick and interactions with deities, and in our conceptualization of love.

Without Hod, our lives and relationship to the world around us would be chaos. In Netzach, as we'll discuss in the next chapter, different flavors of energy become distinct. They then acquire forms and labels in Hod, then become dense enough in Yesod for us to encounter. Hod is where language and communication are born, and it is the sphere of labels and names, where we catalog, sort, and understand differences between things.

I have a lot of Virgo in my natal chart, so for me it's obvious why the name *Glory* would apply to this highly organized sphere. I have always dreamed of owning my own library card catalog. Give me a label maker and lots of little places to store various objects, and I am a very happy human.

Hod is about the glory of the moment when you've finally solved a nagging problem. I chase that exact dopamine rush by solving tough sudoku puzzles. It's about the glory of education and communication, without which humanity would be deeply stuck. It's about passion for teaching and passion for connecting concepts together.

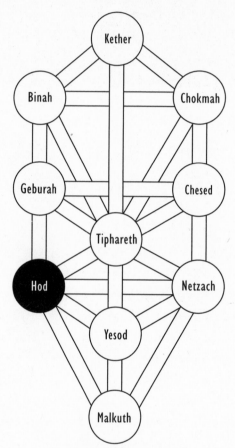

Figure 15: Hod

All occult symbols, including the Tree of Life glyph itself, originate in Hod. It is also the sphere in which we anthropomorphize our deities. Deities are distinct streams of energy, and we are able to relate to them by putting "clothes" of understandable forms on them.

When we talk about ceremonial magick, we're talking about putting energy into a specific, ritualized container to get a result. A magickal container is formed with words, correspondences, symbols, gestures, chants—each piece playing a part in manifesting that which is needed from the ritual or working. As the center for language, labels, and knowledge, Hod gives us the tools to create the container, while Netzach, the seventh sphere, provides the energy.

Words are containers for ideas, and Hod is where words come from. Words have tremendous power, not just in ritual and spellwork, but also in our daily life. One of the most important lessons of magick is that *your words matter*. If spells are part of your practice, the act of casting a spell is you exerting your Will on the universe through your thoughts and words. You say a thing, therefore it is true or will become true. But if you make a habit of lying, hiding the truth, or not meaning your words in your day-to-day life, why should the universe listen to you in ritual or spellwork? We must choose our words carefully, which involves training ourselves out of certain societal niceties that may have become ingrained into our behavior patterns. Insincerity runs rampant in American and much of Western culture, and most of us take it in stride or participate in it willingly. For example, many of us say, "We should get together!" when chatting with an old friend when we both know we're probably not going to make the time to get together. I'm guilty of telling someone I'll send them a book recommendation or a recipe, then forgetting to do so. Lots of people fail to meet deadlines they've agreed to. These things may seem completely inconsequential, and in mundane life they usually are, but if you want the universe to listen to you, you need to work to eliminate these habits from your life. To strengthen our magick and raise our awareness of the power of words as containers of ideas and power, we must avoid dishonesty to others and to ourselves. And that includes stopping saying unkind things to ourselves, like "I'm never going to meet someone I love" or "I'm so hideous" or "Nobody likes me," because these things simply aren't true.

Not only do words matter, but names are incredibly important. Everyone's name is a shorthand identifier for that person and all the things that person is. If you're having a conversation with somebody about a mutual friend, you don't usually have to go through a full description of who that person is because you both understand that name means that specific person.

There are themes throughout fairy tales of gaining power over a thing by knowing its true name. Those with chronic illness, like myself, recognize the power of knowing the name of that illness. It offers you a helpful shorthand to discuss it with doctors, to find support groups, and to search effectively for answers to questions about treatment, lifestyle changes, and more. Without that name, it can be a haphazard journey through online medical sites that may contain little to no helpful information. During my many-years-long quest for a diagnosis, I burst into tears in a doctor's office when she told me my tests for a variety of illnesses came back negative. She was so confused, saying, "But you don't *want* to have these things. They're awful!" She didn't understand that negative tests meant I still didn't have a name for my illness, which meant I'd have to continue flailing in the dark. I needed to know the name of my dragon before I could fight it.

JOURNALING EXERCISE
Pay Attention to Your Words

It's important not to be too hard on yourself while doing this exercise. We live in a culture where insincerity is extremely common. This exercise is meant to help you become more mindful of what you say, not to make you perfect.

For a week, keep a small notebook with you or a note file on your phone, and keep track of some of the things you say to others and to yourself. When you catch yourself saying something hyperbolic or exaggerating, even for comic effect, write it down. When you catch yourself lying, write it down. When you catch yourself being insincere, write it down. When you are confident you are being honest and forthright, write it down. This is a tough exercise—it's okay if you don't catch everything or even most things! You may need to set a regular reminder to stop and think about the things you've said over the past couple of hours. At the end of the week, look at the things you've written and think about how you can improve the integrity of your words.

JOURNALING EXERCISE
The Story of Your Name

Spend some time journaling or recording yourself talking about your name. Some questions to consider: If you still go by your birth name, do you know the story of how you were named? Why was that name chosen? Are you named after anybody, and if so, who? Why did you or those who named you choose that person's name? Did you or those who named you consider any other names? How do you feel about those names they didn't choose?

Do you like your name? Why or why not? What does your name mean to you? If you were to choose a different name, what might you choose and why? If you have a magickal name or nicknames, consider the meanings behind those as well. Are these names important to you, and if so, why? How much of your identity is in your name?

What Makes Hod Queer?

As part of the Queer Identity Triangle, Hod represents the importance of names and labels for gender and sexuality as well as the importance of feeling connected to your name and pronouns as they relate to your gender identity. When you find a label that matches your gender and sexuality, it unlocks new possibilities of self-awareness and discovery. It's suddenly easier to find information about your sexuality and gender and to find other people who share your sexuality or gender. And those of us who have transitioned our gender from the one assigned at birth know how painful it is to have a name that doesn't match our gender identity, and how conversely euphoric it is to take on a name that *does* match.

Like other spheres on the tree, Hod's gender identity is a mixture of inconsistencies. It is also the most explicitly intersex and asexual/aromantic sphere on the Tree.

Hod is peak *both-and* in terms of sexual identity, a meta-sex that is beyond the binary. Its Hebrew name is masculine, yet it sits firmly at the base of the Feminine Pillar. Its planetary connection is Mercury, named for the Roman counterpart of the Greek deity Hermes, who is seen by some scholars as bisexual and androgynous.[35] Further, the child produced by Hermes and Aphrodite was Hermaphroditus, a deity with both male and female sex characteristics, which is the root of the now-outdated term *hermaphrodite*.[36] Drawing from this story, Hod's magickal image is a person with visible breasts and a penis: an intersex person.

The term *intersex* is used to describe people without clear-cut physical indicators of birth sex, whether that is unclear genitalia (such as an enlarged clitoris or having both a penis and vaginal opening), sex chromosomes in a combination like X0 or XXY, androgen insensitivity syndrome, or other factors. Scientific estimates suggest one to two people in one hundred are born intersex in the United States—about the same percentage of people born with red hair.[37] Despite how frequently people are born intersex, however, intersex people of all ages are stigmatized, and many intersex infants have unnecessary surgeries performed on them that result in long-term negative health consequences.[38] Intersex people are everywhere, and if you're not already familiar with the challenges intersex

....

35. Lindsay River and Sally Gillespie, *The Knot of Time: Astrology and the Female Experience* (New York: Harper & Row, 1987), 77.

36. "Hermaphroditos," Theoi Project, accessed May 14, 2021, https://www.theoi.com /Ouranios/ErosHermaphroditos.html.

37. "What Is Intersex?," Planned Parenthood, accessed January 26, 2021, https://www .plannedparenthood.org/learn/gender-identity/sex-gender-identity/whats-intersex; "Intersex," United Nations Human Rights: Office of the High Commissioner, accessed October 13, 2020, https://www.unfe.org/wp-content/uploads/2018/10/Intersex-English.pdf.

38. "Intersex," United Nations Human Rights.

people face in our society, I recommend embracing Hod's passion for research to gain more understanding.

There is no part of the Tree without passion, and the passion of Hod is that of learning not only about the world but about other people. Hod is the sphere of deep friendships and platonic love, particularly the kind of love built from shared intellectual interests. Hod is about passionate relationships or aspects of relationships that are not sexual or romantic. The word *passionate* gets too often tied up in sexuality and romance, but you can passionately love someone or something in a completely nonsexual and non-romantic way. Asexual and aromantic people may feel a particular kinship with this sphere.

Asexuals and aromantics are a broad spectrum of people with complex attractions and behaviors regarding sex and relationships. While some asexual people prefer to avoid sex entirely, other asexuals have and enjoy sex, they just don't experience sexual attraction in the same way others do. Similarly, some aromantic people prefer to avoid romantic partnerships, whereas others enjoy romantic partnerships but don't experience romantic attraction in the same way others do. And there are a large number of variations and nuances of identities in between. The important thing is that aromantics and asexuals are not broken: their sexuality does not need fixing. And because their sexuality differs from the cisheteronormative ideal, asexual and aromantic people are part of the queer community.

In cisheteronormative culture, people extol romance and sex as deeply important parts of everybody's lives, often at the expense of other relationships. Popular culture tells the story again and again of how someone can only find happiness and worth when they find a long-term romantic partner. And there's a prevailing notion that once you find that partner, they must be everything to you—your best friend, your primary emotional support, your ever-present companion so you never have to feel lonely, your financial safety net, and your perfect sexual partner, and they must stay with you until one of you dies. Unfortunately, holding this ideal is both unrealistic and unhealthy. No one person can fulfill all your needs all the time. And the really unfortunate thing is that heterosexual, masculine-identified people in our culture are taught to keep their friendships very shallow and only turn to their feminine romantic partners for emotional support. Once a romantic relationship ends, they face an emotional crisis without a support network they can trust to help them through it. It's a cruel trick of patriarchy to reinforce this self-defeating notion that masculine people having platonic emotional connections is "unmanly."

Hod encourages you to take a queer lens to a culture that normalizes this kind of unrealistic and harmful romantic relationship ideal by remembering that many people in your life can fulfill many important emotional needs. Romantic or sexual relationships are not a requirement for a happy, healthy life, and platonic partners and friends are just as important as romantic or sexual partners. Much as every part of the Tree of Life is divine, our friendships, our connections with mentors and students, and our passion for learning are wonderful things in our lives that must not be undervalued.

Pathworking to Experience Hod

You may record this pathworking and play it back for yourself, have a friend read it, or read it and then walk through it based on your memory. I recommend keeping a journal and pen or recording device nearby so you can write about, draw, or record yourself speaking about your experience immediately after you complete the pathworking. Remember that you are in control of what happens here, and you may end up diverting course from what I've written. It's okay to do so!

Sit comfortably in a place where you will not be disturbed for the next fifteen minutes.

Close your eyes. Take three deep breaths, slowly, in and out. With each exhalation, let go of any tension you find in your body.

Without opening your eyes, visualize the room around you. Now picture it filling with a gray mist, starting at the floor and working its way up to the ceiling until the only thing you can see is grayness. As the mist dissipates, you find yourself in a field sitting on a small wooden platform colored olive, citrine, russet, and black. It's dark, but there's a glow at the horizon—it's either just after sunset or just before sunrise.

In the sky, near the horizon, you can see a bright, yellowish dot you know to be Mercury. As you gaze at it, the platform you're sitting on begins to move toward it. The field and its sounds and smells fade into the distance as you ride the platform, slowly rising higher in the air, flying over forests and hills, until you gradually leave the atmosphere and are flying in space. You can breathe normally and are unafraid of the height—the platform feels stable and secure.

As Mercury grows larger in your sight, you feel your mind suddenly racing, analyzing aspects of its features and location in the sky and all the correspondences you know for Mercury. You think of Hermes, the caduceus, winged shoes, communication. Words and symbols flash through your mind like lightning, and suddenly you are surrounded by an orange mist, obscuring your view.

When the mist dissipates, the platform and Mercury have vanished, and you find yourself in a vast library with orange shelves going in every direction, higher and further than your eyes can see. The air smells a bit musty, like old books, and the floor is composed of pearl and azure tiles, each inscribed with a different symbol. You recognize some as runes, some as astrological symbols, some as alchemical symbols, some as abbreviations from the periodic table of elements, but the rest are a mystery to you. The sheer size of the library and the amount of knowledge it contains boggles your mind.

A person walks around a bookshelf to your left and greets you. They're wearing rich orange robes and have a stack of books under one of their arms. They explain that they are the librarian here and bow in welcome and respect. You bow in return and notice that you feel an instant kinship with this person, a desire to pick their brain about any number of subjects.

Your host leads you to a corner where there is a small café. They offer you a hot drink and some cookies, and you accept. Setting their stack of books on a table, they retrieve your snacks and drinks, and you both sit in soft leather armchairs. "So," says your host. "We're here in this vast house of knowledge. Knowledge is gained and discoveries are made by making connections between different ideas. I want to talk to you about *your* connections for a minute."

Your host makes a complicated gesture, and in the air above your heads appears a vast diagram of people connected with lines. You recognize a small image of yourself in the middle, and all the lines and points emanating from that image represent your family, friends, professional networks, casual acquaintances, and others. You notice there are different types of lines connecting you to the other people. They appear to indicate the quality and type of the connection.

Your host points at the diagram. "When we step back and analyze things, our relationships can look a lot different," they say. "Look at the lines. Which of these relationships feed you and which ones drain you?" Look at the diagram and answer.

(Pause.)

Your host nods. "Is there anything you see here that surprises you?" they ask. Answer them.

(Pause.)

Your host nods again. "Is there anything you need to do to strengthen any of your connections so that they are more nourishing and less draining?" asks your host. Answer them.

(Pause.)

Your host clears your empty plates and cups and leads you to a corner of the library, where you see lots of colorful books on display. "Please take one of these and let it guide you in the days and weeks ahead," your host says. Examine the display and choose a book. Note the title and any images that appear on the cover.

(Pause.)

When you've chosen your book, your host guides you to an elevator. You notice the floor of the elevator is the same wooden platform you took to get here. They bid you farewell, and you thank them for their guidance and the gift. You get into the elevator and the doors close. The night sky surrounds you. You think on what you have learned as you zoom back through space, Mercury appearing once more and growing smaller and smaller until it's just a dot near the horizon as you glide safely back down toward the field. You make a soft landing and get off the platform. You gaze at Mercury one last time, whispering a thanks for the experiences you've had.

Eventually, the air around you fills with a pearly gray mist until you can no longer see the field. When the mist dissipates, you find yourself seated comfortably once more. Take a deep breath, wiggle your fingers and your toes, and when you are ready, open your eyes. If you have any thoughts or impressions from this pathworking you wish to remember, write or draw them in your journal, or record yourself speaking about them while they're still fresh in your mind.

Bringing It All Together

Hod reminds us of the value of all the relationships in our lives, particularly the non-romantic and nonsexual ones, and helps us cultivate a passion for learning. As the sphere of communication, labels, and categories, it also reminds us of the power of our words; helps us put words to our sense of gender, sexuality, and self; and creates the ritual containers necessary to create magick. The wild energy to go into those ritual containers comes from Netzach, the next sphere.

Netzach: The Very Concepts of Gender and Sexuality

Netzach is the seventh sphere on the Tree of Life. It sits at the base of the Masculine Pillar, also known as the Pillar of Mercy or the Pillar of Force, positioned directly across from Hod. Its name means *Victory*, which can be confusing! We'll get to that in a minute.

The dark green color of Netzach brings to mind wild, hot jungles as well as wild, hot passion. It is a lower reflection of the energetic explosion of Chokmah, at the top of the Pillar of Force, and as such, its nature is to be effusive, expansive, and full of energy. It represents emotion, particularly passionate, romantic love and lust: its planetary correspondence is Venus. It also represents artistic creativity. You know that spark that hits you, that moment of inspiration when you have an idea? That's Netzach.

On a more cosmic level, Netzach is where the single force of divine energy descending the Lightning Flash differentiates into different streams and flavors of energy, like light hitting a prism. When those individuated streams get to Hod, they are anthropomorphized and named so that they become accessible for us to work with. We call these streams of energy *deities, divine beings, elements, elementals,* and *spirits.* Reflecting back to the section on polarity in chapter 2, Netzach is a great example of how there are *lots* of different ways to interpret energy, not just *masculine and feminine.*

Netzach's position and function on the Tree of Life are part of why I struggle with the idea of a goddess-and-god or lord-and-lady pairing of ultimate sources of power. Despite the fact that there's gendered imagery associated with each sphere on the Tree, the power to differentiate energy

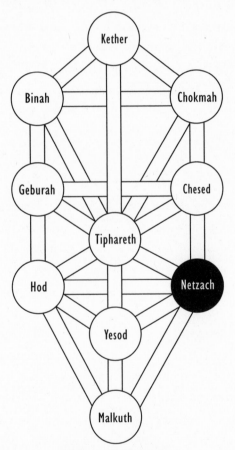

Figure 16: Netzach

streams with any sort of concept like *gender* doesn't exist until we get down to Netzach. If we want to work with the power of Kether, the point of ultimate unity, the source of all, we find that it is genderless. And even if we look at Chokmah and Binah, which sit directly below Kether and have been thought of as the ultimate masculine and ultimate feminine powers on the Tree of Life, their forces are so primal and abstract that they are also beyond the concept of gender. This agender, unified stream of energy continues down to Netzach, at which point we are close enough to manifestation to begin to separate out different streams of energy.

As I noted in the previous chapter, Netzach works with its neighbor Hod to produce magick. Hod provides the structure, but Netzach provides the wild force of energy that brings things into manifestation. Magick simply isn't possible without both these spheres at work.

Netzach and Hod are lower reflections of Chokmah and Binah, but with a lot of added flavor. Where Chokmah and Binah are the concepts of force and form at their most abstract, Netzach and Hod are those concepts at their most concrete and understandable. Hod is not just about the potential for form, but about categories, shapes, names, containers, labels, and groups of things. Hod is about specifics, not generalities. Similarly, Netzach isn't about a general sense of endlessly moving energy, but rather the more concrete concepts of fire, passion, inspiration, creativity, and love. It is primal and sensual. Netzach is the emotional fuel that drives us. It is our Will. It is our motivation.

Why is the sphere called *Victory*, though? The Qabala is full of delicious puzzles like this. I'm sure you've heard the phrase "Love conquers all"—well, that is a victory for love, and Netzach is the sphere of love. Netzach is also the place where artists and creators get the drive to put their ideas out into the world: a victory over their own self-doubt. I think of Netzach in terms of the victory of reconnecting with our more primal selves—the sticky, dirty, playful, happy, id-driven children we once were until our wild emotions and instincts were tamed by society. As we progress up the Tree of Life, it is important to reconnect with that aspect of ourselves, for there is great power and wisdom in that wild, primal part of ourselves. Finding our wildness buried beneath all those carefully honed, civilized, acceptable, people-pleasing shields we've built up over the years is hard work, though. Awakening and connecting with our primal selves in a sustainable and healthy way is a difficult process because along the way, we're likely to unearth parts of ourselves we don't like very much, yet we must accept that they are a part of us.

Another way of phrasing this is in order to become our better, more whole selves, we must gain victory over and unbecome the things we are not: the inauthentic things others taught us to be. We'll discuss this more in Geburah, the sphere where we release the things that don't serve us. Netzach is our inner source of energy and passion for life, the fuel for the difficult journey of unbecoming, as well as our connection to our most authentic, primal selves.

JOURNALING EXERCISE
Considering Your Magick

If spellwork or ritual are part of your regular practice, consider the aspects of Netzach and Hod present in those works. Which parts of your spell or ritual are containers and which parts are energy? What kind of energy do you put into your workings? Write examples in your journal or record yourself talking about them.

What Makes Netzach Queer?

The concept of queerness wouldn't exist without Netzach, because Netzach is where the energies of gender and sexuality become distinct. Doesn't get much queerer than that! Energy becomes differentiated in Netzach, and then these differentiated genders and sexualities get their labels in Hod.

Netzach is the third part of the Queer Identity Triangle, and Netzach is responsible for the way you *feel* your gender or your sexuality. Most of us know our sexuality based on what sexually attracts us, but what does it mean to *feel* your gender? I think about this question a lot because most of the time, I just don't feel like any gender at all. *Feeling* one's gender goes beyond noticing your genitals and deciding they define you a certain way. It's about personally identifying with a concept and feeling it in your bones. Ask yourself, particularly if you're cisgender: Without devolving into gender stereotypes or anatomy, what about you makes you *feel* like your gender? If your genitals disappeared mysteriously one day, would you still feel like your gender? If so, why? It's worth pondering, even if you haven't previously questioned your gender before.

Whatever your gender identity is, and whatever the gender identity of your crush is, Netzach is the burning passion you feel for that person. While the vast majority of the depictions of passionate love in popular culture are heteronormative, part of the toxic underbelly of heteronormativity is society's muting the expression of those romantic, passionate feelings. Speaking from an America-centric point of view, our Puritan roots show themselves in a general cultural disdain for public displays of affection. We are trained to express love through consumerism: greeting cards and gifts, preferably purchased to drive Valentine's Day sales. I was acutely aware of this when I worked at a Hallmark store during my college years.

Bucking the cultural repression of expressions of affection is inherently queer, even if you're straight! In expressing your love in an honest and passionate way, you're subverting cultural expectations of heteronormativity. This is reflected in the early 2000s slang term "to be gay for someone," which translates, either ironically or sincerely, as "to be head-over-heels for someone." To honestly express your deep love for someone is, in many ways, very queer.

Many other aspects of Netzach are super queer as well. Netzach has many components that are masculine—its Hebrew name, its position on the Masculine Pillar, and the fact that it's a lower reflection of Chokmah's endless, projective energy. And yet, Netzach is aligned with Venus, and its magickal image is that of a beautiful, naked woman. To me, this stands as proof that there is nothing specifically masculine about projective energy or the Pillar of Force. The passions of Venus are every bit as overflowing with energy as the nonstop, unfocused excesses of Chokmah and are every bit as magickally powerful. And if someone tries arguing that Venus isn't actually feminine, or that *Venus embodies the masculine principle*, they are both missing the point and hinting at the toxic idea that passionate sex drives are the province of masculine people. Netzach can be simultaneously masculine and feminine, with neither aspect negating or overruling the other. More importantly, Netzach is queer, and the very concept of queerness comes from Netzach.

Pathworking to Experience Netzach

You may record this pathworking and play it back for yourself, have a friend read it, or read it and then walk through it based on your memory. I recommend keeping a journal and pen or recording device nearby so you can write about, draw, or record yourself speaking about your experience immediately after you complete the pathworking. Remember that you are in control of what happens here, and you may end up diverting course from what I've written. It's okay to do so!

Sit comfortably in a place where you will not be disturbed for the next fifteen minutes.

Close your eyes. Take three deep breaths, slowly, in and out. With each exhalation, let go of any tension you find in your body.

Without opening your eyes, visualize the room around you. Now picture it filling with a gray mist, starting at the floor and working its way up to the ceiling until the only thing you can see is grayness. As the mist dissipates, you find yourself in a field sitting on a small wooden platform colored olive, citrine, russet, and black. It's early evening, with the sun just setting.

In the sky, toward the horizon, you can see a bright dot, like a star—but you know it to be the planet Venus. As you gaze at it, the platform you're sitting on begins to move toward it. The field and its sounds and smells fade into the distance as you ride the platform, slowly rising higher in the air, flying over forests and hills, until you gradually leave the atmosphere and are flying in space. You can breathe normally and are unafraid of the height—the platform feels stable and secure.

As Venus grows larger in your sight, you begin to feel the heat of passion rise within you. A range of wild, strong emotions unfurl near your navel and your heart as you travel. Suddenly, you find yourself surrounded by a green mist, obscuring your view of the planet.

When the mist dissipates, you find yourself in a rainforest. It's humid, and you begin to sweat instantly. The air feels as though it's full of steam but also life. The light is dim, as the canopy blocks most of the sunlight. You hear a variety of insects and animals around you and smell damp earth and vegetation rotting and fermenting in the heat. Colorful birds fly around and call to each other from the dense treetops. You begin to pick your way through the huge trees and lush ferns to get a better look around.

"Hello," says a husky, seductive voice near you, and you turn to see a beautiful, smiling, sensual person lounging against a tree a few meters away. They are extremely in their element here, with long, wild, cascading hair and a look of bliss and satisfaction on their face. You're reminded of woodland spirits in Renaissance paintings. The person beckons you to come closer. As you approach, they gently reach out to brush your cheek and gaze into your eyes lovingly. "Welcome. You've met my sibling in Hod, who had many questions and things for you to analyze. Here, I ask no questions. I don't want you to think. I simply want you to feel, to reconnect with the primal forces within yourself.

"Sit down," they say, gesturing at a tree stump nearby. You sit. They stare at you for a moment, then hold their hands in front of you, as if projecting energy toward your lower abdomen. After a moment, you suddenly become aware of a strong, pulsing, warm energy emanating from your tailbone. You feel the building heat of the energy rise in your body, slowly filling the lower half of your torso. You feel a strong urge to laugh, or cry, or shout—perhaps all at the same time!—and then that sensation eases and you simply feel passion coursing throughout your body. Feelings of yearning and confidence and excitement build within you, along with a primal wildness, the desire to run, to chase. You're extremely conscious of the feeling of your heart beating, of the blood pulsing through your veins. It's the most alive you've felt in ages.

(Pause.)

Your host then shifts their hand slightly to point toward your heart. All that passion melts and deepens, and you feel as though feathery wings were tenderly wrapped around you, pouring into you feelings of deep, unconditional, compassionate love and acceptance. You feel safe and cherished and confident that no matter what you do, you will always be loved and understood like this. You feel tears in your eyes, tears of relief and joy and release for being so loved. You want to feel this way forever.

(Pause.)

As you bask in this tender, loving feeling, you realize you wish to share it. You look at your host, who understands the question in your eyes and nods, gesturing you to hold your hands out. "Imagine the person you wish to send love to," your host instructs. "And visualize that feeling as clear green light flowing out of you, from your heart, through your hands, and send it to a bright white ball of energy just above that person's head." You do as instructed.

(Pause.)

When you have finished sending the energy, your host takes your hands gently in theirs and looks deeply into your eyes. You notice their eyes are an extraordinary, deep green that dances and sparkles in the light.

"My gift to you is this," they say, reaching one hand up to lightly touch the middle of your forehead with their finger. You shiver slightly at a delicious sensation that trickles all down your body. It feels as if a tiny, bright little star bursts into existence where they are touching you, and bright, shimmery stardust is coursing through your veins. "This is a spark of inspiration," they say. "Use it well. And remember that which you have felt here, and know you can call those feelings to yourself again."

You blink, and your host has vanished. You realize you are sitting on the same wooden platform that brought you here, and you are once again surrounded by a green mist. When the mist dissipates, you are flying through space, heading back toward Earth. You zoom faster and faster until you break through the atmosphere and then ease back down onto the field where you began your journey. You step off the platform, gazing at Venus one last time, and shivering slightly at the memory of your experience there. You whisper a quiet thanks to Venus for your experience.

Eventually, the air around you fills with a pearly gray mist until you can no longer see the field. When the mist dissipates, you find yourself seated comfortably once more. Take a deep breath, wiggle your fingers and your toes, and when you are ready, open your eyes. If you have any thoughts or impressions from this pathworking you wish to remember, write or draw them in your journal, or record yourself speaking about them while they're still fresh in your mind.

Bringing It All Together

The unbridled, passionate energy of Netzach is the fire and inspiration that fuels our art, our magick, our romantic and sexual relationships, and all things we create. It gives us our innate sense of gender and sexuality before we can put words to those feelings. In our quest for self-discovery, Netzach guides us to claim victory over all the layers of things we *are not* as we remember and honor our most primal, core selves. In doing so, we get closer to a state of internal balance: something we'll learn more about in Tiphareth.

Tiphareth:
I'm Coming Out

Tiphareth is the sixth sphere and is the central point of balance on the Tree of Life. It sits on the Pillar of Balance, or Nonbinary Pillar, at the halfway point between Kether and Malkuth.

Many Qabalists focus on *sacrifice* as the key aspect of Tiphareth, but its name doesn't mean *sacrifice*—it means *Harmony*. I would argue that Tiphareth's core concept is one of balance. Sometimes balance is achieved by sacrificing that which doesn't serve, of course. But sometimes moving or reconfiguring something, or adding something new, brings balance. It's not all about sacrifice all the time. Tiphareth draws its energy from both Geburah (honing and removing excess, metabolizing) and Chesed (vision and expansion), and both of those qualities are reflected in it. Tiphareth is about balancing those energies in the most optimal way.

Balance isn't a fixed state, however. Circumstances change and mandate we be flexible and adapt in order to stay in a state of balance. Tiphareth is, after all, a higher reflection of Yesod, the moon, where we learn flexibility and fluidity. The energy of Tiphareth is not static; it flows.

Your balanced, optimal state looks different depending on your unique circumstances, which change over time. For example, a balanced life for me in my teens would involve balancing schoolwork, a part-time job, my extracurricular activities, my social life, and my health. But in my current life, the concept of balance is much different. Instead of school-work, I have a full-time job. Instead of extracurriculars, I have my band, my coven, and writing blog posts and books. My body and my life need different things in middle age than they needed back then, and finding the balance that works for the moment is a regular juggling act and takes a lot of focus and a lot of saying "no" to things. Moving with the flow as life throws curveballs at you, and being able to readjust priorities and time allocation, is a tremendous asset, and one you can cultivate with the

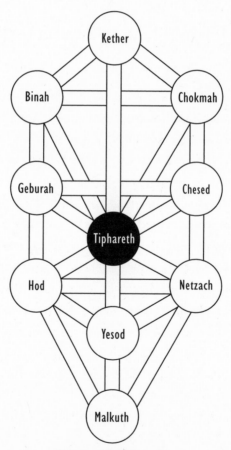

Figure 17: Tiphareth

help of Tiphareth. "Adapt and overcome," as my ex-military friend likes to say. We quickly learn that if you don't devote enough energy to something your body and soul need, you will be out of balance. And if you're not willing to sacrifice anything and try to do everything at max volume all the time, you will burn out.

As humans who depend upon the exchange of money for goods and services in order to survive, money is something we regularly have to balance in our lives. One of Tiphareth's lessons is not to hoard wealth. The movement of resources is the circulatory system of humanity, and it's healthy to keep money circulating—leaving and returning at a regular cadence. To put it another way: If you're lucky enough to live fairly comfortably and have some savings for retirement and for a rainy day, you can keep things in balance by donating money to a cause, using some funds to help out friends in need, or supporting crowdfunding campaigns and small businesses rather than hoarding every spare cent.

Tiphareth's corresponding celestial body is the sun. The sun brings vitality and integration, shines a light on truth, and facilitates healing. Healing, after all, is about restoring harmony, whether physically or emotionally. Interestingly, Qabalists put the sun in the center of the Tree of Life glyph long before it was universally accepted that the earth revolves around the sun!

Another aspect of Tiphareth is that of integrity. *Integrity* is a wonderful word with three meanings: 1. Being true and honest, good to your word; 2. Being complete; 3. Being in optimal condition. All of these ideas align to Tiphareth. The sun's healing aspects can keep us in the best possible condition for our current configuration, and being honorable—in the sense of being good to your word—brings a sense of completion and inner peace. As we discussed in Hod, our words have power, and being true to our word is vital to our magick!

Tiphareth can help you become the best, most optimal *you* that you can be at your current stage of life. Life is full of choices, and while we're confined to linear time and corporeal form, we cannot effectively be and do all the things we or others want us to. We must prioritize and choose, and the energy of Tiphareth can guide us to set priorities and make choices in a way that brings us into better alignment with our potential while maintaining our well-being. It is not about perfection; it's about balance, and it's about what is right for *you*.

In Tiphareth, we can learn to truly love ourselves. Tiphareth's power flows downward into Netzach and Hod, both different expressions of love: romantic and platonic, respectively. The love of Tiphareth is the love of benevolent grace, of truly wanting the best for someone. When you are feeling balanced and happy, you can imagine this kind of self-love as a hug from your higher self.

JOURNALING EXERCISE
Thinking about Sacrifice and Balance

Write a list of ten or so things you are today (athlete, parent, crafter, salesperson, educator, writer, performer, gardener, etc.). Next to that list, write the things you would like to be but aren't: things that are incompatible with your current life circumstances, require more resources or training than you have access to, etc. Spend some time looking at the two lists and consider your feelings about each item. Would you like to move some things from one column to another? Why or why not? What sacrifices would it take to move different things around between lists?

What Makes Tiphareth Queer?

Tiphareth is a reflection of Kether on the Middle Pillar. In Tiphareth, we connect to the spark of the divine and infinite within ourselves, the part of ourselves that is both eternal and genderless. One manifestation of this connection to the infinite is discovering deep inner truths as they exist in our current incarnation.

Tiphareth is part of what I'm calling the Coming Out Triangle, comprised of Tiphareth, Geburah, and Chesed. Each connects with different aspects of the process of coming out as queer. Tiphareth's part of that puzzle is the joy you feel acknowledging your own truth. Geburah and Chesed, which will be covered in the next two chapters, are about the parts of yourself and life that change when you come out.

Remember what I said about Tiphareth being about integrity? Part of the personal-integrity puzzle is admitting who you really are ... to yourself. The integrity of Tiphareth is about the core of our being, literally. If you were to overlay the Tree of Life on the human body, Tiphareth would be where the heart and lungs are—our emotions, our breath, the center of our humanity. These organs keep us in balance with their regular rhythms. While we can survive without an arm or our legs, we cannot survive without the circulating, oxygenated blood provided by the heart and lungs. In a similar way, Tiphareth is the point that keeps the whole Tree of Life in balance, uniting the higher and lower aspects of the Tree and of ourselves.

Most queer people spend some part of our lives not realizing, or at least not admitting to ourselves, that we are queer. I didn't realize I was bisexual until I was seventeen, though the signs were certainly there, in hindsight. I didn't realize I was nonbinary until I was in my late thirties. In both cases, I suffered from lack of vocabulary and visible role models. The only bisexual I knew of as a teenager was Rickie on the TV show *My So-Called Life*, and I didn't identify with him. All my friends considered themselves straight, as far as I knew. And while I've had transgender friends since I was twenty, I didn't know any nonbinary or genderqueer people until my late thirties.

I'm hopeful that having more queer public figures and characters in movies and TV shows will help people figure out their gender and sexuality at a younger age. But even if we have dozens or hundreds of role models, the fact remains that queer identities aren't considered the default in our cisheteronormative society, and most children are raised to understand their identity as cisgender and straight unless proven otherwise. And honestly, digging into the concepts of your own personal gender and sexuality can be kind of an advanced mental exercise. It's not something *all* young children would have an intuitive grasp of, though some do:

there are young transgender kids who absolutely understand their identity at a very early age.

Suffice to say, most of us spend a chunk of our lives either not knowing or not admitting to ourselves that we are queer. That means at some point, there is a shift when we realize that we are, indeed, queer. For many people, this realization is preceded by a feeling that something isn't quite right, something is out of alignment: there's an existential *itchiness* or *abrasiveness* of sorts. Many experience this as dysphoria surrounding their body, clothing, or appearance. Others label this vague feeling as depression or anxiety. Some may experience a full-on mental breakdown as the truth of who they are fights with their preconceived notions of who they think they are. And others may never feel any of these things.

But the awareness, the realization of our queerness, comes with its own set of emotions. There may be panic and fear, particularly if you live with people who may not be supportive. There may be a hefty dose of uncertainty and denial. But there is also often a euphoria that happens when you are able to articulate your inner truth to yourself and again when you're able to align your external self with that inner truth: it just feels *right*.

This feeling of perfect harmony is a Tiphareth experience. You are sacrificing what you are *not* (Geburah) to embrace the truth of who you *are* (Tiphareth) and the possibilities of who you can *become* (Chesed). You are bringing your internal and external selves into harmony. Coming out to yourself is, fundamentally, a healing experience. Coming out to others can be more difficult and is an entirely different process. More on that in chapter 9.

Tiphareth is about becoming the most optimal version of you possible in your current configuration. The most optimal version of you is one that feels right, harmonizes the different aspects of your life, and allows you to be honest with yourself about who you really are. Let the sun of Tiphareth shine on your truth!

Pathworking to Experience Tiphareth

You may record this pathworking and play it back for yourself, have a friend read it, or read it and then walk through it based on your memory. I recommend keeping a journal and pen or recording device nearby so you can write about, draw, or record yourself speaking about your experience immediately after you complete the pathworking. Remember that you are in control of what happens here, and you may end up diverting course from what I've written. It's okay to do so!

Sit comfortably in a place where you will not be disturbed for the next fifteen minutes.

Close your eyes. Take three deep breaths, slowly, in and out. With each exhalation, let go of any tension you find in your body.

Without opening your eyes, visualize the room around you. Now picture it filling with a gray mist, starting at the floor and working its way up to the ceiling until the only thing you can see is grayness. As the mist dissipates, you find yourself in a field sitting on a small wooden platform colored olive, citrine, russet, and black. It's high noon, and the sun is bright overhead in a cloudless sky. Insects are buzzing all around and you feel the heat of the sun on your face.

As you gaze around the field, it suddenly becomes shrouded in shadow. It's an eclipse. The platform beneath you begins to rise straight in the air toward the sun occluded by the moon. You race upward, feeling the platform firmly beneath you, knowing you are not in danger of falling. You see a dark ring in the sky above you and you pass through it, and the moon seems to jump much closer in your sight after you do. You zoom closer and closer to the moon, and then suddenly it seems you pass through it, and the sun is suddenly blindingly bright on your face, growing hotter and hotter as you zoom closer to it.

A golden mist surrounds you, and you find yourself inside a golden, hexagonal hall. The windows are set with crystal prisms casting rainbows on the floor and walls as the light streams through them. The walls appear to be hammered gold, the floor comprised of golden hexagonal tiles. You can hear the haunting melody of a choir harmonizing a beautiful song in a language that is unfamiliar to you. You smell incense wafting in the air. There are comfortable couches covered in rainbow throw blankets and pillows surrounding a firepit in the center of the hall and tables laden with food around the edges of the room.

This is a place of peace and harmony. You feel as if weeks of stress have simply melted off you, and you are able to simply *be*. You are conscious of your breath and your heartbeat.

"Hello," says a voice near you, and you turn to see a person with a shining, golden light surrounding them. They are wearing a golden robe over a simple white tunic. They invite you to sit on one of the couches with them, and you oblige. Glasses of cool water are set before you to drink.

Your host asks you to take a moment to really feel the energy of the space. You take a deep breath and listen to the music of the choir in perfect harmony, smell the incense, and feel soft warmth on your face from the light streaming in from the windows. You realize you feel deeply at peace and very much present in the moment. Everything feels right and balanced. You smile.

Your host nods. "This feeling of peace and balance isn't limited to this place," they say. "It lives within you. There are
many ways to access it when you need to—through breath,
through meditation, through focus. Tell me, how do you
bring small moments of peace into your day-to-day life?"
they ask. Answer them.

(Pause.)

Your host nods. "Have you given thought to what your Great
Work is, your higher purpose in this life?" they ask. Answer
them.

(Pause.)

Your host continues. "It becomes easier to access these feelings of peace and balance when you are leaning into your
purpose, when you are doing your Great Work, when you are
living your truth. I want you to think on these things in the
days to come," they say.

Your host then makes a gesture in the air, and into their hand
appears a shiny, golden coin. They hand it to you. It feels cold
and heavy in your hands. The coin is intricately embossed
with an image on either side that reflects your Great Work.
What do you see?

(Pause.)

Your host says the coin is yours to keep and to consider. You
thank them, and they lead you to the back of the room where
you see an alcove containing the platform you rode in on. As
you get onto the platform, the soft golden light surrounding
your host seems to expand to fill the room and surrounds you
as you stand on the platform. You are once again aware of
the deep peace and balance of this place. You close your eyes
to take it in, and when you open them, you no longer see

the hall but are surrounded by golden mist, which dissipates until you see the stars and the moon in front of you, growing larger and larger until it seems you have passed through it, and then you see the earth again, far in the distance. You pass through the dark ring in the sky again, and the earth grows much larger, and soon you are descending back to the field where you started. You get off the platform, and as you do, the eclipse ends, and the field is bathed in sunlight. You feel the sun's warmth on your skin and whisper a thanks for your experience.

Eventually, the air around you fills with a pearly gray mist until you can no longer see the field. When the mist dissipates, you find yourself seated comfortably once more. Take a deep breath, wiggle your fingers and your toes, and when you are ready, open your eyes. If you have any thoughts or impressions from this pathworking you wish to remember, write or draw them in your journal, or record yourself speaking about them while they're still fresh in your mind.

Bringing It All Together

To achieve the healing, integrity, and wholeness Tiphareth offers, we must be truly honest with ourselves about who we are and regularly adjust the balance of our lives to changing circumstances over time. If different parts of our lives are puzzle pieces, Tiphareth is the experience of all of them clicking together to form the distinct picture of *you,* perfectly in tune with who you truly are. To achieve this state, however, we must unbecome what we are not in Geburah.

9

Geburah: The Pain of Unbecoming

Geburah is the fifth sphere on the Tree, sitting in the middle of the Pillar of Form. Its name means *Might*, and it is commonly associated with war and destruction.

Geburah is well worth considering, particularly in an era where so many people are rightly protesting abuses of power and societal injustices. Geburah is about destruction, yes, but it's about destroying that which does not serve, that which is harmful, and white supremacy, systemic racism, systemic ableism, systemic queerphobia, systemic transphobia, systemic sexism, and other unjust systems and abuses of power cause harm, period. The actions of protestors and activists are Geburic actions.

Geburah is about standing up for justice. It's about not allowing corrupt systems to continue. It's about enfranchising the disenfranchised and ensuring everyone has autonomy and a voice. The Stonewall riots in 1969 were a Geburic action, for example. I wrote this chapter near the end of a year that, particularly in the United States, was marked by stunning abuses of power, both by law enforcement officials and by elected officials. A silver lining of this situation was that many people woke up to the reality of systemic tyranny and realized their previous lack of awareness was due to their privileged status. Lots of people took action, working to ensure the voices that needed to be heard, were heard. May they continue to do so long after the atrocities stop getting as much media coverage.

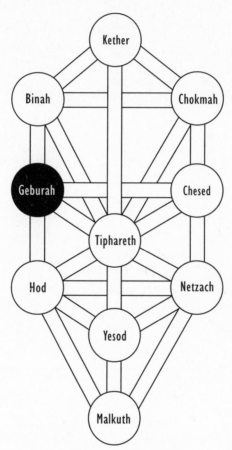

Figure 18: Geburah

Geburah is not about wanton destruction or cruelty. Those using destruction to prop up the status quo are not aligned with Geburah. Those oppressing other people and those who use the power of ludicrous wealth to escape justice for committing humanitarian abuses are not aligned with Geburah. Its name is *Might*, not *Might makes right*.

Geburah is not a bully, but rather is the "Celestial Surgeon," to quote Dion Fortune.[39] It's where we learn our hardest but most valuable lessons, and where lasting change happens.

On a macro level, Geburah is the metabolism of the universe. Many of us were taught to value creation over destruction, yet one could not exist without the other. A world in which things are endlessly created would get impossibly crowded. Likewise, a world with nothing but destruction would be barren. These two forces are parts of a necessary anabolic/catabolic cycle, like how plant waste breaks down to become compost, then enriches the soil to grow new food.

Want more analogies? Here we go.

White blood cells perform Geburic action within your body, fighting off dangerous infections. Geburah debunks falsehoods (think *MythBusters*) and laughs at tyrants to humble them (think *Saturday Night Live*). Geburah is your personal trainer or life coach, helping you develop the discipline needed to achieve your goals. Geburah is the editor that makes the manuscript really sing, and, unfortunately, it's also the rejection letter when you've still got more work to do. Geburah tells you to stop getting distracted and just do the thing already. Geburah is a protector of the vulnerable.

I like to think of comic superhero Squirrel Girl as a perfect example of the powers of Geburah in action. Squirrel Girl often wins her battles by talking to and empathizing with those who are committing crimes or attempting to consume the earth, and she attempts to resolve the root cause leading them to a life of crime or planet consumption. There's a brilliant panel in one issue where she's smiling and propping up a book called *So You've Discovered Some Significant Downsides to Late-Stage Capitalism* for a tied-up, masked bandit to read, teaching him how to improve his finances so he doesn't have to steal anymore.[40] Squirrel Girl is a force for Geburah.

. . . .

39. Dion Fortune, *The Mystical Qabalah* (San Francisco: Weiser, 1998), accessed April 7, 2021, loc. 2683 of 5850, Kindle.

40. Ryan North and Erica Henderson, *The Unbeatable Squirrel Girl, Issue 19*, in *The Unbeatable Squirrel Girl Vol. 6: Who Run the World? Squirrels, Issues 17–22* (New York: Marvel Comics, 2017).

JOURNALING EXERCISE
Finding Geburah

Spend some time journaling or recording yourself talking about the impact of Geburah in your own life. Some ideas to consider: a time when you didn't get something you wanted but things turned out for the better because of it, a goal you achieved because you applied great mental or physical discipline over a period of time, a lesson you learned the hard way, a surgery or other medical experience that removed something causing your body harm, painful truths that helped you become a better person, a breakup that paved the way for a better relationship afterward, or a time when you worked for justice in the world. How did your life change because of these experiences? Did you realize at the time that these experiences were beneficial, or were you caught up in the pain? How has your view of these experiences changed over time?

What Makes Geburah Queer?

In the previous chapter on Tiphareth, we noted Tiphareth's part of the Coming Out Triangle is the euphoria of coming out to yourself, of realizing and beginning to live a more authentic life. But in order to live more authentically, there are some things you have to let go. Geburah is about unbecoming what you're not in order to make room for the potential of who you can become.

Unbecoming is not an easy process. Many people who come out as queer are faced with uncomfortable choices when they realize their identity: *Do I tell my family/friends/boss, or do I live a lie to maintain those relationships at status quo? Am I willing to let go of the image of myself I've had for so many years, an image built up and supported by those around me of what I look like, how I act, who I date, whether I date at all? What if everyone hates me? What if nobody understands? I don't want to be alone. What if I'm wrong, and I'm not this way at all?* Complicating this, coming out isn't a onetime occasion. You may come out to yourself multiple times in your life as your understanding of yourself changes and deepens. And many of us in the queer community have to repeatedly come out to new people in our lives, as most people assume heterosexuality and cisgenderism are the norm.

Even if you've spent your whole life surrounded by queer people, it still takes a tremendous amount of courage to come out to others. Courage is also a Geburic trait! Many queer people face very real consequences for coming out. Beyond the inherent difficulties of processing the question "Who am I now?" many queer people encounter unsupportive or downright hostile family and communities. And depending on where you live, your rights may be severely restricted or your life may be in danger if you're openly queer. For these reasons and many more, do not *out* people or pressure them to come out before they're ready. Respect people's autonomy to find the right time for themselves, if they decide to come out at all.

For those who choose to come out to themselves and those in their life, there are rewards as well as new challenges. One of those rewards is to reimagine possibilities for yourself. More on that in the next chapter, when we talk about Chesed.

Beyond its coming-out associations, Geburah gets bonus queer points for being one of two genderfluid spheres on the Tree of Life. It is known by two different Hebrew names: Geburah (feminine), which means *Might;* and Din (masculine), which means *Judgment.*

Pathworking to Experience Geburah

You may record this pathworking and play it back for yourself, have a friend read it, or read it and then walk through it based on your memory. I recommend keeping a journal and pen or recording device nearby so you can write about, draw, or record yourself speaking about your experience immediately after you complete the pathworking. Remember that you are in control of what happens here, and you may end up diverting course from what I've written. It's okay to do so!

Sit comfortably in a place where you will not be disturbed for the next fifteen minutes.

Close your eyes. Take three deep breaths, slowly, in and out. With each exhalation, let go of any tension you find in your body.

Without opening your eyes, visualize the room around you. Now picture it filling with a gray mist, starting at the floor and working its way up to the ceiling until the only thing you can see is grayness. As the mist dissipates, you find yourself in a field sitting on a small wooden platform colored olive, citrine, russet, and black. It's night, and you can hear crickets, cicadas, and other night insects buzz and chirp around you. It's warm and humid.

You look at the starry night sky and notice a red dot toward the horizon. It's Mars. As you gaze at it, the platform you're sitting on begins to move toward it, skating along the ground and eventually grazing treetops and lifting higher and higher into the atmosphere. The air grows colder as you ascend and you feel your blood boil with determination, strength, and courage the closer you get to Mars. The red planet grows larger and larger until it fills your vision and then you are surrounded by a red mist.

When the mist dissipates, you find yourself in a courtyard surrounded by brick buildings. It appears to be a university. You take a look around, and your eyes fall upon a person wearing red academic robes standing in front of you. "Hello," they say crisply. "Welcome to Geburah. Let's take a tour." They turn and begin walking away. You follow.

"Geburah is where people come to optimize themselves," says your guide. "What is optimal is different for each person, but everybody can improve by letting go of the things that no longer serve them."

You walk past several empty rooms, and your guide gestures at each one briefly to explain what they are. There's a group therapy room, a ritual space, a fashion show catwalk, an art studio, a stand-up comedy space, music practice rooms, a gym, a doctor's office and surgery center, a self-defense classroom, meditation spaces, and more. "All these spaces are where people can let go in some way," your guide explains. "Or help them create healthy boundaries with others or themselves. People cling to self-destructive ideas and habits that keep them from realizing their potential. Here, we help them shed those things. It's often a painful but productive experience. Lifelong lessons are learned here.

"Now," asks your guide. "Which of these spaces would you like to see in more detail?" You find yourself drawn to one of the rooms. What sort of space is it? What do you see? What features stand out to you?

(Pause.)

Your guide asks why you chose that room. Answer them.

(Pause.)

Your guide may have some wisdom to offer you regarding how this space reflects something going on in your life— something you need to refine or let go of. Listen to what they have to say to you.

(Pause.)

Your guide pulls a gift from their pocket and hands it to you. It is a small, five-sided red box with the words "Send love to *future you*" inscribed on it. "Open it," your guide says. "It contains something that will help you with your goals." What do you find inside the box?

(Pause.)

You thank your guide for the gift and the tour. They bow and walk you back to the courtyard where you began. You step onto the platform you rode to get here. Your guide nods to you, and you are surrounded by a red mist. When the mist dissipates, you are once again flying through space, toward Earth. You contemplate your gift as the earth grows larger in your sight. Soon, you break through the atmosphere, and the air grows progressively warmer as you glide back down to the field where you began. You get off the platform and gaze up at the night sky, offering a silent thanks to Mars for the experience you've had today.

Eventually, the air around you fills with a pearly gray mist until you can no longer see the field. When the mist dissipates, you find yourself seated comfortably once more. Take a deep breath, wiggle your fingers and your toes, and when you are ready, open your eyes. If you have any thoughts or impressions from this pathworking you wish to remember, write or draw them in your journal, or record yourself speaking about them while they're still fresh in your mind.

Bringing It All Together

Geburah is the sphere in which we learn hard lessons and make big changes to become more *ourselves* and work to move society forward, toward equal rights and justice for all. Removing things from our lives we've outgrown, and fixing things in society that harm people, is a painful process. But that process makes room for who we can become with the help of Chesed, the next sphere.

Chesed:
Who Can I Be Now?

Chesed is the fourth sphere on the Tree of Life, sitting right in the middle of the Pillar of Force across from Geburah. Its name means *Mercy*. This is the sphere of vision, planning, imagining what's possible, and working in alignment with your higher purpose.

Chesed is the counterpart to Geburah. Chesed is the upbuilding, while Geburah trims that which isn't needed. They aren't opposites, but rather complement each other in a balanced, eternal cycle, and there are aspects of each in the other's sphere. In Geburah, you can find Chesed in the purpose behind the sacrifices and edits made there: Chesed is the broader vision that drives those changes. In Chesed, you can find Geburah in the eternal dance between what is ideal and what is implementable: the feeling of Chesed is one of yearning for the perfect situation but also being consciously aware that perfect is not practical or doable. It's like wanting to turn your home into a 10,000 square-foot tree house but being aware of your financial, space, and time constraints. Geburah is the quiet voice saying "no" in Chesed, keeping its visions and plans focused on the optimal solution that accounts for practical constraints rather than perfection.

Chesed's powers help point us in the right direction for our own future. Chesed is about living your true purpose, when your Great Work on this plane is aligned with your soul. Its powers are also particularly useful when you're envisioning the future of a group or project.

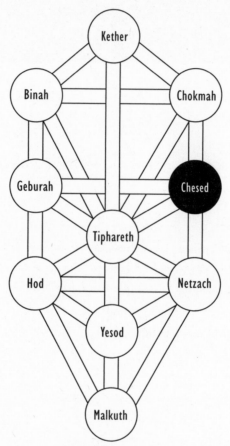

Figure 19: Chesed

If you're organizing a group, Chesed can help you imagine the ways for that group to grow and evolve strategically. I was extremely fortunate that, as I was taking on the mantle of acting high priest of my coven, I was part of a large ritual in which I embodied Chesed. This ritual is performed every few years by the Assembly of the Sacred Wheel. The

Tree of Life glyph is laid out using colored fabric circles in a big outdoor area. Within each circle is an altar to that sphere and a person embodying that sphere. Participants walk from Malkuth to Kether and experience a five-minute personal ritual at each.

The Chesed altar my colleague Mark Pemburn and I designed included a desktop globe, a tetrahedron, and a drawing board with a brush that allowed people to paint an image with water: an image that would evaporate after a minute. Mark and I each embodied Chesed in separate rituals that weekend. Those who approached our sphere were taken through a brief pathworking to acknowledge their power in the world and then prompted to think of something they wanted to change. They condensed that thought down into a simple sigil, which they then drew onto the board to send that thought into the universe.

The ritual was powerful for participants, but it was also transformative for me as a new acting high priest, deepening my relationship with Chesed in my new role. In the weeks that followed that ritual, I was full of ideas, plans, and—thankfully—energy to implement them within my coven. I highly recommend working closely with Chesed if you are in a leadership position, particularly if you're just starting out or need a burst of energy and ideas. I invite you to try the working on page 194 to create a leadership charm using the power of Chesed.

Chesed's powers of leadership and vision help align your actions with your Will. Working toward your personal goals can feel almost effortless when you are acting in perfect alignment with who you want to become. It's like having the perfect job and doing that job every day to the best of your ability because it uses your skills to the fullest and brings you joy— not because you'll get fired if you don't. You become motivated by the satisfaction of doing certain things instead of being motivated by fear of punishment or consequence.

If you are working in alignment with your Will, with the power of Chesed, punishment and shame do not enter into the equation because the work itself feels *so right*. This feeling of perfect alignment is both difficult to attain and maintain, though. When we find ourselves out of alignment, the best thing to do is to forgive ourselves and then pick back up and try again. Remember, the sphere's name means *Mercy*. If we wallow in self-punishment, nothing gets done.

Our best self-care puts us in a mindset of being able to simply do the things that must be done because it feels natural and right to do so. Aligning your actions with your goals, with your Will, is actually liberating. That is the point of all our self-work and, ideally, our dream for society as a whole.

JOURNALING EXERCISE
Thinking about Aligning to Your Will

Spend a few minutes freewriting or recording yourself speaking, without overthinking and without stopping, on the topic of "What is my ultimate goal? What is my Will for my life? What is my higher purpose?" What comes out may surprise you. If nothing comes to mind right now, spend a few nights thinking on this question before you go to bed; see what comes to you in your dreams, then try the exercise again.

When you have a goal in mind, think about what aspects of your life are working in service to that goal and which are not.

What Makes Chesed Queer?

Chesed is the third part of the Coming Out Triangle. Tiphareth is the euphoria of coming out to yourself. Geburah is the hardship of letting go of the parts of you that no longer fit and confronting the prospect of coming out to others. Chesed is the sphere that helps you envision who you can become and how to express the person you've realized you are.

As you let go of the parts of you—and sometimes relationships—that do not fit the person you've realized you are, you make space for new possibilities, for new joys. This is the trying-on-clothes phase of coming out. The energy for this activity comes from Chesed, but the easiest way for us to access that energy is through Yesod, the sphere of imagination. Unlike Yesod energy, though, this isn't just playful: it's play with a purpose and a vision, play that comes with a *plan*.

The power of Chesed is the awe you might feel at your first Pride event. It's your careful examination of the styles of others of your newly understood gender or sexuality and learning from their journeys of self-discovery. It's finding new friends and new communities where you feel comfortable expressing yourself and testing new looks and personas. The power of Chesed is when that amazing, experimental phase of coming out finds a direction. It's about asking who you are and imagining who you could become, and planning how to make that happen. It's about exploring and building a vision of your future and your role in the community, which is a fundamental and positive shift for those who had bleak visions of their future before realizing who they were. Chesed affirms and confirms our deepest and brightest truths, as it contains the pattern for our unfolding evolution. This feeds into that feeling of inner harmony when we realize who we truly are, as discussed in the Tiphareth chapter.

Chesed also gets bonus queer points for being the other genderfluid sphere on the Tree. Like Geburah, it's known by two different Hebrew names: Chesed (masculine), which means *Mercy*, and Gedulah (feminine), which means *Greatness*.

Pathworking to Experience Chesed

You may record this pathworking and play it back for yourself, have a friend read it, or read it and then walk through it based on your memory. I recommend keeping a journal and pen or recording device nearby so you can write about, draw, or record yourself speaking about your experience immediately after you complete the pathworking. Remember that you are in control of what happens here, and you may end up diverting course from what I've written. It's okay to do so!

Sit comfortably in a place where you will not be disturbed for the next fifteen minutes.

Close your eyes. Take three deep breaths, slowly, in and out. With each exhalation, let go of any tension you find in your body.

Without opening your eyes, visualize the room around you. Now picture it filling with a gray mist, starting at the floor and working its way up to the ceiling until the only thing you can see is grayness. As the mist dissipates, you find yourself in a field sitting on a small wooden platform colored olive, citrine, russet, and black. It's night, and there are crickets and other nighttime insects chirping and buzzing around you. The air feels slightly damp and smells of night-blooming flowers.

You gaze up into the starry sky and notice a light tan dot off to your right, which you know to be Jupiter. As you stare at it, the platform you're sitting on begins to move toward it, rising higher in the air and skimming along treetops, higher and higher, until you break through the atmosphere and begin to fly through space.

Jupiter, with its thick red, brown, yellow, and white stripes, grows larger in your sight as you zoom toward it. You feel inspired, and your brain begins clicking with plans and strategy. You feel expansive and aware of a multitude of possibilities. Suddenly you are surrounded by a royal blue mist, and when it dissipates, you find yourself in a dark space, standing on a massive, glowing globe that looks like Earth. At first, you see big blue oceans and greenish-brown blotches of continents, and then you begin to see layers showing cities, patches of farmland, deserts, and so on. You find yourself wishing you could see things up close, and when you make that wish, you feel yourself shrinking down to the point where you can see buildings and roads from high above. You walk around the globe, each step taking you hundreds of miles, none of your steps causing any damage or harm. You are an invisible observer of this world. What do you see?

(Pause.)

A voice greets you, saying, "Hello, and welcome to Chesed." You turn and see a person in royal blue robes wearing a gentle, loving smile, standing a few feet away from you. As you look at them, the globe beneath you becomes a sea of different faces of people. People of all ages, races, and genders appear, some smiling, some angry ... a whole range of emotions is present. You feel a connection to the faces you are seeing, even if you don't know them. After a few moments, your host speaks. "Take a moment to feel yourself as part of an incredibly complex organism called humanity. Every person has a role to play. Every person is important. Can you feel the connections around you? Can you feel how your life and your actions touch those around you?"

(Pause.)

The faces on the globe disappear, and the globe becomes blank. "It may not always seem like it," says your host, "but you have power. You have the power to shape your life, and you have a role to play in shaping the world around you. Feel the gears within you turn, feel the creative force bubbling up within you, and then put that force into a vision. What you visualize will become so beneath your feet. Show me: what would you like your world to look like?" Take a few moments to imagine the world you inhabit as you would like to see it. What do you see, and how does it make you feel?

(Pause.)

Your host smiles at what you have created. Do they have any words of wisdom to share? Listen.

(Pause.)

When your host has finished speaking, they make a gesture in the air that moves you both off the globe and onto a nearby flat surface. They continue to gesture, and as they do, the globe containing your vision begins to shrink down, smaller and smaller, until it's the size of a large marble. Your host plucks it from the air and hands it to you. It feels warm, electric, and bursting with potential. Your host says, "Hold this vision in your heart and think of ways you can make it so." You thank your host; they bow and then vanish. You realize the surface you're standing on is the platform that brought you here. You are once again surrounded by blue mist, and when it dissipates, you are flying through space toward Earth.

You burst through the atmosphere once more, descending through clouds, and gradually come to a gentle stop back in the field where you began. You hear the crickets and cicadas chirping and buzzing and smell the flowers around you. You gaze back at Jupiter and whisper a quiet thanks for the experience you've had there.

Eventually, the air around you fills with a pearly gray mist until you can no longer see the field. When the mist dissipates, you find yourself seated comfortably once more. Take a deep breath, wiggle your fingers and your toes, and when you are ready, open your eyes. If you have any thoughts or impressions from this pathworking you wish to remember, write or draw them in your journal, or record yourself speaking about them while they're still fresh in your mind.

Bringing It All Together

Working with Chesed on a personal level can help you connect to and align with your true Will. When your actions are in harmony with your Will, every choice and effort becomes easier. Chesed's visionary powers are deeply useful in any kind of planning or management situation to help you strive for the optimal future for that project or community. Community is what we'll be focused on next, in the Queer Community Triangle of Binah, Chokmah, and Kether; but before we get there, we have an Abyss to cross: Da'ath.

Da'ath: Writing Your Own Script

Da'ath, which means *Knowledge,* is one of the fascinating complexities of the Tree. It is Schrödinger's Sphere: It simultaneously exists and doesn't. It's a bit like a distant planet that we can't actually observe directly but we can detect based on its gravitational effect on other things nearby. There is no number assigned to it, and the earliest work we have on Qabalah, the *Sepher Yetzirah,* is quite clear that there are ten spheres, not eleven.[41] For this reason, some Qabalists refuse to acknowledge Da'ath.[42] Others theorize that it exists but is not actually on the Tree of Life itself.[43]

Does it exist? Does it not exist? I think the answer to both questions is *yes.* Da'ath is a paradox.

In working with the Tree of Life, you may become conscious of certain *veils* or *membranes*: places where you feel some resistance to ascending, typically resting just below each of the triangles. If you've been

. . . .

41. W. Wynn Westcott, trans., *Sepher Yetzirah* (Brampton, Ontario: Ballantrae Reprint, 1991), 15.

42. Moler, *Shamanic Qabalah,* 83.

43. Penczak, *The Temple of High Witchcraft,* 389.

following the pathworkings for each of the spheres in this book, you'll notice I included a representation of one such membrane whenever you ascend the Middle Pillar: a dark ring in the sky between Malkuth and Yesod. This is the point at which the manifest becomes unmanifest.

Another veil on the Tree has a bit more of a kick to it: the one just beneath the Supernal Triangle on the Pillar of Balance. Da'ath, though, is less of a *veil* and more of a place: a deep, seemingly uncrossable Abyss. If you imagine the Lightning Flash as a road stretching between Kether and Malkuth, Da'ath would represent a point at which the road ends at a cliff and picks up on the opposite side of a yawning crevasse, and you have to figure out how to cross it. In some ways, Da'ath can be seen as a barrier blocking our view of the absolute unity of Kether until we pass through it.

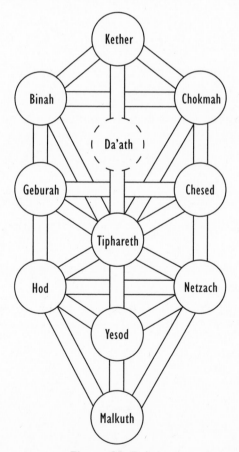

Figure 20: Da'ath

Da'ath is in the empty space in the Tree of Life that seems like it *should* contain a sphere for the sake of symmetry, if nothing else. Some Qabalists believe that Malkuth was in this space until the Fall described in the Book of Genesis.[44] Regardless of the reason behind it, the fact that the Tree has a hole in this spot is significant. That blank spot is a moment of pause, a place of separation. It's a representation of the fact that to reach the Supernal Triangle, you're going to have to leave some stuff behind: in particular, a lot of assumptions about existence.

Da'ath is a breaking point on the Tree. Looking at it in the direction of the descending Lightning Flash, it can be seen as the flashpoint where

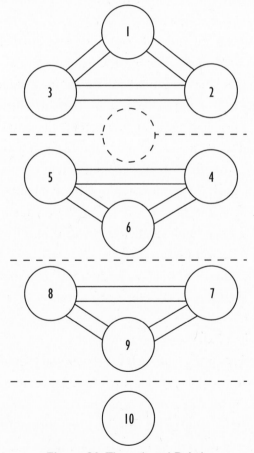

Figure 21: The veils and Da'ath

44. Penczak, *The Temple of High Witchcraft*, 392.

the energies of Chokmah and Binah, endless force and the potential for form, combine and transmute to create the basic building blocks of matter. This follows the same pattern as how the powers of Geburah and Chesed unite and are transmuted in Tiphareth, and how the powers of Hod and Netzach unite and are transmuted in Yesod. As Yesod is the gateway of manifest reality, Da'ath is a gateway to the *concept* of manifest reality.

But if we flip that around and approach Da'ath from below instead of from the top of the Tree of Life, we experience that gateway in reverse. Instead of force and form uniting, we see them separating, breaking down the very concept of reality. In other words, when we ascend to Da'ath, things start getting weird.

Encountering Da'ath is deeply confusing and disorienting. Though Da'ath means *Knowledge* in Hebrew, it represents *all* knowledge. It is the combination of Chokmah (wisdom) and Binah (understanding), after all. But approaching it from our perspective in Malkuth, where those powers are separating rather than combining, it is more like being overwhelmed with information without any sort of context. Approaching Da'ath is like watching a news story from one hundred different perspectives, but not being able to integrate the information to form any kind of cohesive narrative. It would be like reading a PhD-level paper on quantum mechanics before you had taken a single mathematics class: you'd have lots of information, but you'd lack context to make sense of it.

Some see the Abyss of Da'ath as leading to the Qlippoth, or reverse Tree of Life.[45] The Qlippoth is like a photonegative of the Tree, full of hollow shells pretending to be spheres on the proper Tree. If you take a sphere and remove all the aspects that make it productive and divine, that's what the shell of that sphere looks like in the Qlippoth. For example, the Qlippoth would feature Geburah in an aspect of wanton destruction and Chesed in an aspect of tyranny.

Are there lessons to be learned from the Qlippoth? Yes. One can always learn more about a thing by understanding its shadow. But for the

....
45. Penczak, *The Temple of High Witchcraft*, 396.

sake of focusing on a clear, simplified introduction of the Tree of Life, I'm not going to dwell on the Qlippoth, as that territory gets a lot murkier. So let's get back to Da'ath.

The path of the Lightning Flash passes through Da'ath when it travels between Binah and Chesed. This is the one part of the Lightning Flash that separates from the twenty-two paths on the Tree to form its own hidden path. Understanding Da'ath, crossing the Abyss, means finding a way where there appears to be none. For those who have seen the movie *Labyrinth* (1986), when Sarah first tries to enter the Labyrinth to save her baby brother, she is frustrated because she's faced with what appears to be one solid wall with no turns or entrances. She is trapped outside, trying to get in. After a brief chat with a friendly worm, however, she realizes that there are plenty of entrances—she just wasn't seeing them. She was *assuming* it was one solid wall, but when she tries to step into the wall itself, she finds she can pass through after all.[46] In this way, Da'ath is a higher reflection of Yesod, the sphere of illusion. We must confront our illusions—our concept of what is real on the manifest plane—and see past those preconceptions to find the truth.

Da'ath is a liminal space between two types of existence, the boundary between two types of reality. Moving into the Supernal Triangle means we begin to lose key concepts of manifestation: particularly time, our senses, and three-dimensionality. Things become truly archetypal in the Supernal Triangle, to the point where they are difficult for our manifest selves to comprehend. That's part of crossing the Abyss: sacrificing the framework of our manifest reality to be able to experience the places in which form, force, and existence are merely potentialities. The pathworkings on Binah, Chokmah, and Kether will portray these spheres in a way we can more easily imagine and relate to our earthly existence, but these pathworkings are only approximate metaphors for experiences that are very hard to describe in words.

. . . .

46. David Bowie and Jennifer Connelly, *Labyrinth*, directed by Jim Henson (Columbia Tristar: 1986), DVD.

There is no pathworking in this book for Da'ath, because experiencing Da'ath on its own, rather than as a place between other spheres, carries too much risk for those who are new to the Qabala. If you are new to Qabala and want to continue exploring and learning more about Da'ath, I encourage you to do more study and work with the Tree of Life to prepare yourself for such a journey.

But I will take a moment to look at Da'ath through a queer lens, because I simply can't resist.

JOURNALING EXERCISE
Leaps of Faith

Spend some time journaling or recording yourself speaking about metaphorical leaps across or into the Abyss. Think of times when you had to be brave and trust in an uncertain outcome when making a change. In what circumstances is it risky to be yourself? When have you had to take an action on faith alone? When have you had to let go of something you believed to be true and dramatically shift your perspective in order to make progress? What have you gained from these experiences?

What Makes Da'ath Queer?

Approaching the Abyss of Da'ath, we are like Miles Morales in *Spider-Man: Into the Spider-Verse*, standing on the precipice of a tall building, about to jump, unsure if we'll be able to catch ourselves. We must find the path that doesn't exist, step out into open air, and trust that we won't fall to our doom.

> **Miles Morales:** *When will I know I'm ready?*
>
> **Peter B. Parker:** *You won't. It's a leap of faith. That's all it is, Miles. A leap of faith.*[47]

. . . .

47. Shameik Moore, Jake Johnson, and Hailee Steinfeld, *Spider-Man: Into the Spider-Verse*, directed by Bob Persichetti, Peter Ramsey, Rodney Rothman (Sony Pictures: 2018).

In a similar way, queer people make this leap of faith when we come out, when we leave the house expressing a gender different from the one assigned to us at birth, or when we kiss a same-gender partner in public. Authentic existence means facing our fears daily and hoping that we won't be punished for daring to be ourselves.

In my school days, I was regularly accused of being "weird." It was the number one insult hurled at me by my classmates in Minnesota, where the predominant culture deeply values conformity. For example, in Minnesota, when someone wants to say they don't like something, they will say it's "different," which is a polite way of saying something is *bad*. *Weird* became my unwitting brand early on, and my occasional attempts to conform to the mainstream were mocked with laughter. If I had not been bullied in this way, I never would've believed anything was different or shameful about me. But instead, I was repeatedly made to see myself through the cruel and judgmental eyes of my peers.

I don't know what exactly changed to shift my mindset on this. Honestly, it may have been my avid watching of *Mystery Science Theater 3000*, a show produced in Minnesota that frequently satirized the idea of conformity.[48] But one day, sometime in my mid-teens, I realized, "Hey, you know what? I *am* weird. And that's something I *like* about myself." This is part of why I like using *queer* as my personal identifier—it also means "weird." This is when I found my strength: when I started to look at myself through my own eyes, with my own vision of what I wanted to be, I liked the uniqueness of what I saw and embraced it.

That moment of realization, though small, was me finding a path across the Abyss that didn't seem to exist before. It was me taking a leap of faith. When I ended up making more friends after this realization because I was suddenly more confident, I realized that I didn't fall.

Being queer is scary, particularly for those whose queer identities aren't well-represented in public media, and even more so for non-White people, people who have disabilities, people who live in regions that write

....

48. Leah Schnelbach, "8 Lessons MST3K Taught Me About Writing, Life, and Everything," June 26, 2013, https://www.tor.com/2013/06/26/life-lessons-from-mystery-science -theater-3000/.

persecution of queer people into their laws, people who live in poverty, and people who struggle with mental health. If the triangle of Geburah, Chesed, and Tiphareth is the Coming Out Triangle, the point of Da'ath represents that moment of taking a deep breath and being yourself, and finding others who are like you. Our dominant culture gives us a variety of scripts for how to be a White heterosexual cisgender person and repeats those scripts in books, video games, TV shows, movies, and advertisements—all the mass media that surrounds us. There aren't a lot of available scripts for being queer, however; too many Hollywood movies and TV shows end a queer character's story at the moment of coming out, as if that were the main goal of any queer person's life, which doesn't give us a lot to work with in terms of modeling what our lives can be like *afterward*. Part of the fear of coming out is the fear of having to make up our own script—the fear of defining who we are with words we may not yet have. The feeling of knowledge dissolving in Da'ath is the feeling of throwing away the straight, cisgender script, picking up a blank book, and beginning to write our own—or realizing we don't need a script at all.

Da'ath, the sphere that is not a sphere, Yesod on a higher arc, compels us to question what is true and what is real, including the very concept of scripts for life that we must either follow or create. Our knowledge is so flawed and incomplete in this manifest reality bound by linear time and location; there's so much to experience in this universe beyond that which is physically available to us. And the great joke of it all is that most of what we think is really important to know, to understand, or to be, isn't important at all in the grand, cosmic scheme of things. The unmaking of knowledge in Da'ath hints at the pure, profound unity of Kether above it: we are all one. The challenge here, from a queer perspective, is to acknowledge that we are all united in community without erasing our individual experiences and identities, which *do* matter on this manifest plane and in our day-to-day lives.

As you ascend the Tree of Life, you continually transform yourself. The transformation at Da'ath is a one-way trip: Once you see through the illusions of manifest reality, you are forever changed. In the same way, once you realize you are queer, there's no way to reverse your knowledge of that.

Bringing It All Together

Da'ath is the Abyss where knowledge either incorporates or dissolves, depending on which way you approach it. It's the breaking point between the parts of the Tree of Life that are easier to understand from our perspective in manifested reality and those that are simply ephemeral potential. When queer people come out, we throw away the standard "how to be" script, which brings us across the Abyss. Our actual and our potential selves become one.

To better understand our potential, we must connect with others, and so we continue our ascent into the Queer Community Triangle, starting with Binah.

Binah: Understanding Queer Community Sorrow

Binah is the third sphere on the Tree of Life, sitting at the top of the Pillar of Form. Its name means *Understanding*. Binah needs to be understood both in terms of its pillar and in relation to the other spheres in the Supernal Triangle—the top three spheres on the Tree. Working down from Kether, Binah is the first point on the Tree where the potential exists for form. The spheres that precede Binah are pure unity and potential (Kether) followed by pure energy (Chokmah). Binah takes that potential and that energy and does something with it: it gives it shape.

As energy flows down the tree, following the Lightning Flash, it performs a beautiful dance between potential, limitation, and balance before it becomes manifest in Malkuth: like one long editorial process before a book is published. As we look at the Pillar of Form as a whole, we see a common thread of *limitation*. In Hod, we see the need to categorize, organize, and name things so that we may communicate about them. Saying what a thing *is* grants it power, but also defines what it *is not*, and therefore puts a limit upon it. In Geburah, we see the need to remove things that aren't needed to achieve balance—again, placing a limitation. In both these spheres, limits are placed on things so that their function may be enhanced, and that theme of limitation begins in Binah, where *form as a concept* is expressed.

Binah, Chokmah, and Kether—the first three spheres on the Tree—work in concert, almost like a machine. These spheres perform the initial, needed steps toward manifestation by first defining manifestation as a concept: *Things can exist. We need energy and forms to make them.*

Starting with Kether, we see raw, inert potential—the idea of a thing before the concept of an idea could even exist, because there is nobody to have the idea. From that potential, we go to Chokmah, which is a limitless

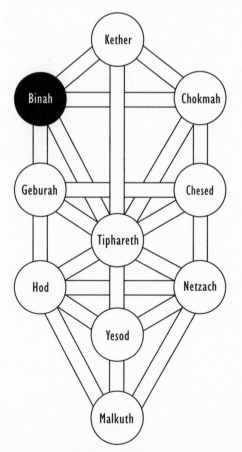

Figure 22: Binah

outpouring of energy with no container. From that endless energy, we go to the potential for form, which is Binah.

When considering the relationship between Chokmah and Binah, a popular metaphor is that of a steam engine. An engine with nothing to move the parts accomplishes nothing. Steam, with no container, has nothing to push against, and all that energy amounts to nothing. But if you funnel the steam through the engine, you create movement and therefore power. Binah is the engine, and Chokmah is the steam. Energy and form need each other.

But the engine is, of course, a metaphor here. Nothing is manifest until it reaches Malkuth at the bottom of the tree, and as we get into the top three spheres on the tree, things become a lot more abstract. The potential for form in Binah can be likened to atoms—the building blocks to become form, without being form as we experience it from our perspective in this reality.

Binah is the third sphere. If you think of each sphere adding a point of dimension to a drawing, Kether is a single point, Chokmah is two points that form a line, and Binah is three points that form a triangle— the first shape. But three points only gets you a *two-dimensional* shape. In *A Wrinkle in Time* by Madeleine L'Engle, the main characters have the experience of being pulled through a two-dimensional place, where they cannot survive.[49] In the same way, Binah suggests form and shape, but manifestation and life are not yet possible. Binah is the equivalent of a quickly scribbled sketch of a three-dimensional object. It's a hazy outline suggesting form, but has neither depth nor form itself.

As one of the Supernals, Binah is cloaked in mystery. The color associated with the sphere is black, and as you'll discover in the pathworking, it's hard to work with sensory metaphors to experience Binah. Binah is known for being dark and mysterious, and many of the symbols associated with it are dark and mysterious things, like the deepest depths of the ocean, dark caves, and the mysteries of birth and death. If that last part

....

49. Madeleine L'Engle, *A Wrinkle in Time* (New York: Square Fish/Farrar, Straus and Giroux, 2012), 76.

sounds familiar, you'll note that Binah's assigned color, black, is also one of the four colors of Malkuth, which is also known as the Gate of Death. The death associated with Binah is much more abstract, however.

A sphere's energy and action changes depending on the direction from which it is approached, particularly in the Supernal Triangle. If we look at Binah from the perspective of energy flowing down from Kether and Chokmah, we see Binah turning energy into the potential for form. But conversely, when approached from the spheres below it, Binah is where potential for form and matter is transmuted back into energy. Binah is, therefore, a sphere of both life and death, working on a more archetypal level than Malkuth's Gate of Death. After we take that leap across the Abyss, not knowing if we'll fall or fly, we find ourselves in a place before three dimensions, where there only exists energy and an idea of where to put it.

In moving from Da'ath to Binah, we lose knowledge and gain understanding: a paradox we started to ponder in the previous chapter. Understanding also means compassion, so Binah is a sense of compassion unhindered by what we believe is true. It's pure, unconditional empathy. Knowledge—particularly incorrect information or beliefs—sometimes gets in the way of our compassion for others. Unlearning bad information and eliminating unconscious biases can be more valuable to gaining understanding of a person or thing than acquiring new knowledge.

JOURNALING EXERCISE
Darkness and the Unknown

Spend some time journaling or recording yourself speaking about the concept of darkness and the unknown. Write or say as many words and associations as you can, not worrying if they are right. Then consider what you've written or recorded and write or say how each word makes you feel in the context of darkness. Are you afraid of darkness and the unknown? What about darkness and the unknown is scary? Can you think of instances where you've ventured into darkness and found something valuable from the experience?

What Makes Binah Queer?

Binah and Chokmah are both feminine names in Hebrew, so I like to think of them as the lesbian power couple that sits atop the Tree of Life. Traditional Qabalists may crap their pants at this descriptor, as Chokmah and Binah are often held up as being the supreme divine masculine and feminine, respectively, but there are actually clues in the Bible that indicate they both represent feminine forces. I noted in the introduction that I'm not fond of biblical overlays on the Tree of Life, but this one is particularly queer, so I'm hoping you'll let it slide. Chokmah, which means Wisdom, and Binah, which means Understanding, are personified, feminine figures who speak in the Old Testament, particularly in the book of Proverbs.[50]

> *Hear how Wisdom lifts her voice, and Understanding cries out. She stands at the cross-roads, by the wayside, at the top of the hill.*[51]

In addition to being one half of the lesbian power couple atop the Tree of Life, Binah is also queer because much of what it represents is forbidden and taboo. Binah is associated with the dark and mysterious aspects of that which has been often ascribed to the feminine: childbirth (and, by extension, sexuality), the womb, death, the near-infinite depths of the sea, darkness, and silence. And as a sphere of birth and death, Binah is often associated with the underworld as well.

Why are these things considered taboo? Because our society fears that which it does not understand. So yes, though Binah's aspects are largely aligned with things ascribed to the feminine and it sits atop the Feminine Pillar, which makes it seem very cisheteronormative at first glance, the taboo experience of Binah has strong parallels with the queer experience.

The queer experience of Binah and Chokmah together is a more meta version of that which occurred between Geburah and Chesed. Geburah was about letting go of parts of your old self and life that no longer fit

· · · · · · · · · · · · · · · ·

50. Pollack, *The Kabbalah Tree*, 88.

51. Proverbs 8:1–2 (*The New English Bible with the Apocrypha*), quoted in Pollack, *The Kabbalah Tree*, 88.

after you come out, and building the courage to come out at all. Chesed was about exploring the possibilities of who you can become after you come out. Binah and Chokmah are those experiences on a higher arc: our communal experiences of sorrow and exuberance within the queer community.

As mentioned earlier in this chapter, *understanding* also means *compassion*. Experiencing compassion in a world full of pain is, by definition, experiencing pain and suffering. The impact of the AIDS crisis in the 1980s and 1990s, which killed nearly an entire generation of gay and bisexual men, is still felt deeply by the queer community today. We grieve the loss of friends, family, and potential elders, and are furious at the intentional neglect by people in power who could have prevented such a massive death toll, but chose instead to ignore or politicize the epidemic. And in a more recent example, one of the urgent requests circulated on social media in light of the protests against police brutality in 2020 was for White people to educate ourselves on systemic racism. The process of learning about the atrocities committed against Black people by White people throughout history is painful but necessary. Binah is associated with sorrow and grief for the pain in the world—the sorrow and grief that can motivate us to listen and take action for a better world.

As we celebrate the civil rights gained for people of color, queer people, women, disabled people, and others, we grieve those in our communities who have died, those who have been and who still are tormented and silenced, on the pathway to getting us those rights. We have lost so many lives to hatred, bigotry, and systemic and societal neglect and abuse. Our communities do not exist in isolation. Every marginalized person's rights are important and must be fought for. We all need to examine our unconscious biases and the ways in which we perpetuate systems that oppress others so we can work together to fix this mess.

In 2020, a friend said to me, "I'm so tired of everybody being so angry." To which I countered, "I'm so tired of having so many reasons to be angry, sad, hurt, frustrated, and appalled." It is a tremendous privilege to feel as though anger is optional because it means the horrors are not upon your very doorstep. Ignoring problems, or *just thinking positive thoughts* will not make them go away. We can't fix systemic racism, sexism, homophobia, ableism, transphobia, or queerphobia with "thoughts and prayers," nor can we fix them by simply being angry or terrified all the time. Our feelings are like the endless energy of Chokmah: powerful but useless unless we put them to use. Binah understands our anger, our fear, and our pain and offers the ability to take those emotions as fuel and transmute them into action.

In experiencing Binah in a queer context, we acknowledge those who came and fought before us, who paved the way for our lives today. We acknowledge the pain caused by systemic discrimination and hate, and in acknowledging the pain and the suffering, we become motivated to do something about it.

Pathworking to Experience Binah

You may record this pathworking and play it back for yourself, have a friend read it, or read it and then walk through it based on your memory. I recommend keeping a journal and pen or recording device nearby so you can write about, draw, or record yourself speaking about your experience immediately after you complete the pathworking. Remember that you are in control of what happens here, and you may end up diverting course from what I've written. It's okay to do so!

Sit comfortably in a place where you will not be disturbed for the next fifteen minutes.

Close your eyes. Take three deep breaths, slowly, in and out. With each exhalation, let go of any tension you find in your body.

Without opening your eyes, visualize the room around you. Now picture it filling with a gray mist, starting at the floor and working its way up to the ceiling until the only thing you can see is grayness. As the mist dissipates, you find your-self in a field sitting on a small wooden platform colored olive, citrine, russet, and black. It's night, and as you gaze up into the sky, you see many stars and the new, dark moon. You see a yellow-brown dot that you know to be Saturn high overhead.

As you stare at Saturn, the platform you're sitting on begins to rise into the air and move. You zoom toward the planet, with its beautiful, orange rings. It gets closer and closer, and then you are surrounded by a black mist, obscuring your view.

You expect the mist to dissipate, to show you something, but your vision stays dark. You are in an extremely dark, silent place, though you can feel a slight rocking, as if you were on the deck of a ship, and smell an ocean nearby. You look around, hoping to see something. Eventually, your eyes adjust to the darkness and you can see the faint outlines of waves churning in the distance. You're still unsure where you are, but you have some sense of horizon now.

As you gaze out into the ocean, you hear a faint whisper in your mind. "Welcome to Binah," says the voice. And then the floor drops from beneath you, and you are falling, fall-ing, falling until you splash into the ocean, and then you sink down, deeper, deeper, spinning and turning. You can breathe underwater, but you can no longer see even faint outlines. Your senses no longer mean anything. You feel the bound-aries of yourself and the water around you begin to dissolve. Your senses are gone. There is nothing to hear, nothing to see, nothing to smell or taste, and only the sense of cool water surrounding you. It is the barest sense of existing.

(Pause.)

The infinite ocean surrounding you is unknowable and vast. You hear that faint whisper in your mind again. "In this moment, you do not need your senses. Let go of what you think you need to know, to see, to feel."

(Pause.)

As you release, you begin to notice that there is more than nothingness concealed within this vast ocean. You don't know exactly *how* you know, but you become aware of other beings in the depths. You are not alone, but nothing here means you any harm. You remember that life on Earth began in the sea. You think of the first sea creature that crawled onto land. You think of beginnings . . . and then you think of endings.

(Pause.)

As you think, the voice whispers in your head once more. It has a message just for you. Listen.

(Pause.)

Eventually, you float to the surface of the ocean, and when you reach out, you touch a circular wooden platform. You climb onto it and are instantly surrounded by a black mist once more. When it dissipates, you are surrounded by the starry sky—stars that seem blinding now in comparison to the darkness where you were. You zoom back down toward Earth. You break through the atmosphere, and soon you see the trees and the field, and the platform softly touches down onto the grass. You step off the platform, then look up to the sky at Saturn, sending it a silent thanks for your experience.

Eventually, the air around you fills with a pearly gray mist until you can no longer see the field. When the mist dissipates, you find yourself seated comfortably once more. Take a deep breath, wiggle your fingers and your toes, and when you are ready, open your eyes. If you have any thoughts or impressions from this pathworking you wish to remember, write or draw them in your journal, or record yourself speaking about them while they're still fresh in your mind.

Bringing It All Together

Binah gives us the potential for form, which is also the potential for birth, death, and beginnings and endings in general. As the sphere of understanding, it challenges us to educate ourselves about and honor those who have suffered and those who still do suffer in the fight for rights and justice for all. Shared understanding of civil rights history and current injustices should move us to take action for a better future.

Communal sorrow is, unfortunately, a core part of the queer experience. But, as poet Kahlil Gibran wrote, "The deeper that sorrow carves into your being, the more joy you can contain."[52] In the next chapter, we'll look at the experience of queer community joy.

52. Kahlil Gibran, "On Joy and Sorrow," Poets.org, Academy of American Poets, accessed April 11, 2021, https://poets.org/poem/joy-and-sorrow.

Chokmah:
Pride Energy

Chokmah is the second sphere on the Tree of Life, sitting at the top of the Pillar of Force. Its name means *Wisdom*. If you think of Kether as a big, cosmic switch in the *off* position (all potential, but nothing happening), Chokmah is what happens when that switch is flipped *on*. It's an explosion of pure energy in every direction, unorganized and uncompensated. It's like a bright light filling a space with no end. It's not until Binah, the third sphere, where that energy has the potential for form.

As we discussed in the previous chapter, if you consider Kether to be a single point, Chokmah is the addition of a second point that the first point projects to in order to form a line, which suggests movement. Chokmah is about unending motion and expansion, like the universe following the big bang. It's the burst of energy that can be a catalyst for change. Its energy is stimulating and energizing. It is pure force without form, boundaries, or anything to push against.

The explosion of energy of Chokmah is often compared to ejaculation: the metaphorical endless, fertile seed spewing from the great cosmic phallus, creating the universe. I prefer to compare Chokmah's energy to the more generic concept of an unending orgasm, as opposed to specifically phallic ejaculation. After all, people with penises are not the only ones capable of orgasm—or ejaculation, for that matter.

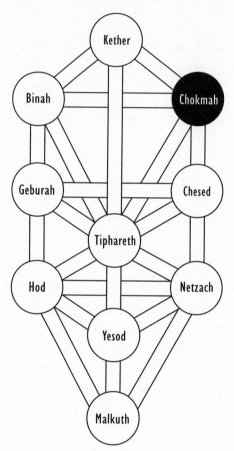

Figure 23: Chokmah

The reason why I prefer the more gender-neutral *orgasm* concept here is partly because we as a society need to move away from the idea that penises are the main expression of fertility. But also, using an ejaculation metaphor to describe Chokmah's energy is imprecise at best. Ejaculation is fluid moving in basically one direction from a container. Since Chokmah's energy is more like an explosion of excitement in all directions from no particular source, I think it makes more sense to think of full-body orgasmic sensation as an analog to Chokmah's energy: that every-nerve-is-on-fire,

I-could-probably-power-six-cities-with-the-intensity-of-this-feeling type of climax. *That* is Chokmah.

I'll also reiterate that the energy of fertility is not limited to sexual procreation or sexual orgasm, as we've explored previously. It can also be the energy of creative pursuits. That outburst of energy you feel when you hit upon a great idea and want to make it into a reality? Chokmah energy. The feeling when something really amazing happens and the world seems full of endless possibilities? That's Chokmah. It's stimulating, it's catalyzing, it's exciting.

Moving backward up the Lightning Flash, from Binah to Chokmah we experience the dissolution of form, leaving nothing but pure energy. Intriguingly, there are sacrifices to freedom made no matter which direction you go. When form is gone, suddenly all restrictions are gone. You are truly free … yet incapable of doing much of anything with that freedom. Extreme amounts of uncompensated energy do nothing but move. When energy encounters form, it loses the freedom to be anywhere and everywhere all at once, but gains the freedom to accomplish things. In polytheism, many believe deities work through humans because deities are incorporeal—they can't do anything without tangible form. Chokmah is the second sphere, and the number two implies collaboration. Energy must be embodied or in some way restricted to be useful. Chokmah needs its counterpart, Binah, as much as Binah needs it. Without the energy of Chokmah, Binah would be inert.

As the sphere that means *Wisdom*, Chokmah serves as a companion to Binah, which means *Understanding*. The distinction between these two concepts, and the interplay between them, is worth meditating upon, particularly in relationship to Da'ath, which means *Knowledge*. If we think about knowledge as a vast info dump of data without context, understanding would help us contextualize it, and wisdom would help us act upon it. If you were handed a spreadsheet full of numbers, with Binah you could understand what those numbers mean, and with Chokmah you could have the wisdom to figure out next best steps based on that data. But when Chokmah is operating without Binah or Da'ath, we have wisdom without knowledge or understanding. What does that feel like? To me, it's the awareness of beginnings: the sense of Kether, the point of pure potential, and the hint of what that potential could become. It's being in touch with the unity and source of all in a way that is hard for us, as manifested beings, to comprehend.

Wisdom is both the first thing that occurs after the great cosmic switch gets turned on and also the last experience before returning to pure unity. The experience of wisdom in descending the Tree is one of *Wow, there can be things!* Or, rather, *I've seen the potential of all things in Kether. We can make stuff, which can do stuff, so let's use some energy to make some things.* The experience of wisdom climbing the Tree is the flip side of this: *Things do not matter, and our separate, incarnate existence is an illusion, because all is one.*

This kind of thinking is a paradox: How can things be so important and worth creating and yet not matter? There's a line in the TV show *Angel* in which the lead character says, "If there's no great glorious end to all this, if nothing we do matters, then all that matters is what we do. 'Cause that's all there is. What we do. Now. Today."[53] To put it another way: We're manifested for a reason. We need to experience the here and now to really live on this plane because our embodied existence is fleeting. If none of it matters in the end, we may as well enjoy the ride and make it meaningful, while making the ride as enjoyable and meaningful as possible for others too.

JOURNALING EXERCISE
Consider Excitement

Spend some time meditating, then drawing, recording yourself speaking about, or journaling on the concepts of excitement, stimulation, and catalyst. What do these words mean to you? Think of some times when you felt really, truly, I'm-going-to-burst-at-the-seams excited.

53. Thomas J. Wright, dir., *Angel*, season 2, episode 16, "Epiphany," aired February 27, 2001, on WB Network.

Moments when you felt you had boundless energy. Times when you felt like a light bulb had just turned on, and suddenly there was an explosion of possibilities in your brain. How would you describe that feeling? What happened after you had that feeling? Did your actions change how you felt? Why or why not?

What Makes Chokmah Queer?

Chokmah is traditionally aligned with All-father deities—Odin, the Dagda, and Zeus, for example—and held up as a concept of pure virile masculinity. But as I said in the previous chapter, I like to think of Chokmah and Binah as the lesbian power couple at the top of the Tree of Life because both are feminine names in Hebrew. It's not just the names, though. There are other feminine connotations for Chokmah. Let's look again at the Book of Proverbs for some clues.

In Proverbs 3 and 8, Wisdom and Understanding (Chokmah and Binah) are represented as feminine mythological figures, Wisdom being the consort of God who helped develop creation. The way in which Wisdom, Chokmah, is described mirrors the way in which we see things come into manifestation along the Lightning Flash path—Chokmah is Kether's co-creator, watching the dance of force and form, expansion and limitation, as the world is created:

Wisdom's Part in Creation
The Lord created me at the beginning of his work,
the first of his acts of long ago.

Ages ago I was set up,
at the first, before the beginning of the earth…
when he marked out the foundations of the earth,
then I was beside him, like a master worker;
and I was daily his delight,
rejoicing before him always,

rejoicing in his inhabited world
and delighting in the human race.[54]

Going beyond the Bible, the Greeks also personified Wisdom as a goddess, called Sophia. And the study of wisdom—philosophy—or philo-Sophia, means "the love of Wisdom."

All this to say, there's a strong argument to be made that the ultra-masculine, super-virile Chokmah is really an all-powerful feminine force, who is occasionally seen in drag.

As I mentioned in the previous chapter, the experiences of Binah and Chokmah are the community manifestations of the Geburah and Chesed *Coming Out Triangle* experiences. In the case of Chokmah, we can sum up the bombastic expansion and celebration of the wild energy of queerdom in the word *Pride*.

In Chesed, which sits directly below Chokmah on the tree, we explored the joys of considering our personal potential after coming out. At Pride, we celebrate that which we are, what we have survived, and where we could go *as a community*. We celebrate the strides made for civil rights. We join together to show the world we are unashamed of who we are, and that we are everywhere. As we just discussed, Chokmah is the exuberant revelation that there can be things, along with the realization that those things are a fleeting illusion. So, to that end, we're here—manifested; we're queer—expressed individuality that was mere potential in Kether; we're community—we're gathered, acknowledging the strides we have made together. We are individuals who recognize our ineffable connections to each other: connections that not only create community but create movements for social change. We celebrate because community joy gives us fuel to keep fighting for our civil rights.

At its best, the energy of Pride is effusive and exuberant, bursting with activity, rainbows, creativity, new connections, and joyful reunions. It's colorful, wild, and uplifting. I feel the energy of Chokmah when I am on the dance floor at Pride, twirling around in a wild outfit, wearing

....
54. Proverbs 8:22, 23, 29–31 (NRSV).

face paint and glitter, reveling in the joys of feeling myself and everyone around me feeling themselves, dancing and sweating and singing along to loud disco music. I am in the moment, connected to my life force, and energetically connecting to those around me. It's effervescent, it's primal, it's bliss.

Boisterous Pride celebrations aren't everyone's cup of tea, of course. The more introverted or just plain exhausted members of our community can certainly celebrate the spirit of Pride in ways that are more authentic to them. The important part of Pride is the recognition that you are part of something bigger than yourself, and that together we can build upon the work done by those who came before to keep making this world a better place for future generations.

Pathworking to Experience Chokmah

You may record this pathworking and play it back for yourself, have a friend read it, or read it and then walk through it based on your memory. I recommend keeping a journal and pen or recording device nearby so you can write about, draw, or record yourself speaking about your experience immediately after you complete the pathworking. Remember that you are in control of what happens here, and you may end up diverting course from what I've written. It's okay to do so!

Sit comfortably in a place where you will not be disturbed for the next fifteen minutes.

Close your eyes. Take three deep breaths, slowly, in and out. With each exhalation, let go of any tension you find in your body.

Without opening your eyes, visualize the room around you. Now picture it filling with a gray mist, starting at the floor and working its way up to the ceiling until the only thing you can see is grayness. As the mist dissipates, you find your-self in a field sitting on a small wooden platform colored olive, citrine, russet, and black. It's night, and as you gaze up into the sky, you see many stars and the full moon. You feel drawn to a faint dot in the starry sky, which you know to be Uranus.

As you stare at Uranus, the platform you're sitting on begins to rise into the air and move. You zoom toward the planet, a hulking gas giant of light blue-green. You rush toward it until you are surrounded by a pearly gray mist.

When the mist dissipates, you find yourself in a space with no defined shapes, just very bright light that seems to come from everywhere. You feel ... warm, and oddly fizzy, efferves-cent. The feeling builds; you feel hotter and hotter, and the vibration gets more intense. You feel like your whole body is vibrating at a super-high frequency. And then ... you burst apart. Every molecule of you dissolves and you become pure energy, joining a rushing current of energy that is everywhere at once, swirling and moving incredibly fast. Enjoy this feel-ing, this chaos of nonstop movement, for a moment.

(Pause.)

What does it feel like to no longer have form? To no longer have limits?

(Pause.)

Does this experience have a message for you? Listen.

(Pause.)

Slowly, you feel yourself begin to re-form, bit by bit, particle by particle. All the pieces of you rejoin into the whole that is you until you are once again complete.

(Pause.)

You find yourself sitting on the circular platform. The brightness surrounding you fades, and you are again surrounded by pearly gray mist. When the mist dissipates, you are surrounded by stars. You zoom back through space, down toward Earth. You break through the atmosphere, and soon you see the trees and the field, and the platform softly touches down onto the grass. You step off the platform, then look up at the fuzzy, tiny dot of Uranus in the sky, sending it a silent thanks for your experience.

Eventually, the air around you fills with a pearly gray mist until you can no longer see the field. When the mist dissipates, you find yourself seated comfortably once more. Take a deep breath, wiggle your fingers and your toes, and when you are ready, open your eyes. If you have any thoughts or impressions from this pathworking you wish to remember, write or draw them in your journal, or record yourself speaking about them while they're still fresh in your mind.

Bringing It All Together

Chokmah's energy is an explosive, effervescent orgasm: the same vibe as a bombastic Pride celebration, when we come together to celebrate our individuality and our unity. The wisdom of Chokmah is both the discernment needed to start the process of creating that which is mere potential in Kether and also the perspicacity to understand that separation is an illusion, and all things are one. Let's conclude part 2 by examining that unity in more detail in the next chapter.

Kether: The Queerest of the Queer

We began at the end, and we end at the beginning. The highest point in the Tree of Life is actually the root of all that the Tree becomes.

Kether, which means *Crown*, is the first sphere on the Tree of Life. It represents the ultimate unity and potential of all things and the source of everything expressed in the Tree.

The obvious reason for the name of the sphere, *Crown*, is simply its location at the top of the Tree. But if we think more deeply on this concept, a crown is not the head—it sits *above* the head. Kether is the beginning before the beginning, the moment before the first spark of creation. It is the source of all, but the source of all is inert potential. You can think of Kether like a silent inhalation before speaking, singing, or chanting. It's the universe getting ready to do something. Kether is like a strand of DNA into which the whole universe is encoded. It is the roadmap, or organizing principle, of what that thing can become. It's the laws of physics without being the expression or examples of those laws. This is part of why we say, "Malkuth is in Kether, and Kether is in Malkuth." Malkuth is the manifested potential of Kether.

Ivo Dominguez Jr. likes to say that Kether is like a USB flash drive containing the file of a movie. Looking at the flash drive in the palm of your hand is not the same as watching the movie, yet the movie is still contained within it.

As noted in previous chapters, Kether is a single point—an excellent representation of both ultimate unity and ultimate potential. The experience of Kether is one of absolute peace, nothingness, and stillness. It is an experience in which we are no longer individuals, but are reunited with the cosmic consciousness.

It is not, however, perfection. It is potential for all—for good, bad, and everything in between. It is everything that could be, and everything that will not be, all bundled up together. It is everything and also

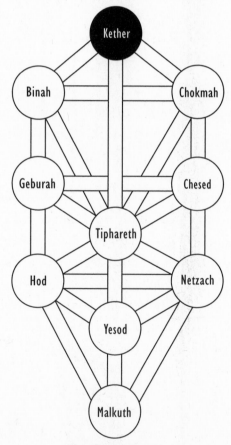

Figure 24: Kether

nothing, as the sphere that is the opposite of manifestation. A Qabalist's bumper sticker might say, "In Kether, all things are possible."

Approaching the Qabala from an occultist's perspective, we see the spheres on the Middle Pillar as representing layers of consciousness. Kether sits at the top of this pillar and represents the highest level of consciousness attainable. We move our consciousness from this plane in Malkuth, up to the level of the imagination and collective unconsciousness of Yesod, up to the place of harmony and balance in Tiphareth, cross the Abyss of knowledge in Da'ath, and finally arrive at a place of ultimate unity and dissolution of the Self—something we can't truly do in our current, incarnated state. The best we can do is catch glimpses of Kether's power while we are manifested.

It's important to remember that the energy of Kether is contained within all the other spheres on the Tree. Its energy moves to form all the spheres, paths, and pillars below it, changing as it moves but still retaining its blueprint and original spark throughout the journey. You can also think of this relationship in simple mathematical terms: Kether is the first sphere, and every other number is divisible by the number one. We could even see the three pillars in the glyph, all of which emanate from Kether, as being extended versions of the numeral 1. In a similar manner, Kether's assigned color is *brilliance*—pure, shining light. Without light, we wouldn't be able to see the colors represented by the other spheres.

Kether is our root, our source. Kether connects us to one another and to the universe and reminds us of the part of ourselves that is eternal. As part of my daily magickal practice, I begin my morning with a self-blessing using scented oil to scribe a pentacle on my forehead while saying, "I am a child of starlight." I don't remember consciously choosing this particular phrase—it just seemed natural one day, and I rolled with it. But the more I thought about it, the more I realized this blessing serves as a reminder of that brilliance that is the source connecting us all. In this blessing, I acknowledge the Kether within me and my connection to the universe.

⌒⌒

JOURNALING EXERCISE
Your Personal Kether

Spend some time meditating, then record yourself speaking or write in your journal about your personal Kether. Some questions to think about:

1. Where within your personal energy field do you feel a spark, a brightness? It may be in your body or slightly outside yourself. There are no wrong answers here.

2. Can you play with that spark or brightness? Can you make it larger? Smaller and denser? Can you move it around?

3. Can you feel a connection through that point? What happens if you try to travel along that brightness?

4. Can you ask that brightness for advice?

What Makes Kether Queer?

The magickal image for Kether is of a bearded king in profile. Modern Qabala scholars point out that showing a masculine character in profile hints at the flip side being feminine in nature, showing this sphere as a higher reflection and source of the combined powers of Chokmah as divine masculine and Binah as divine feminine.[55] This idea is another one of those aspects of the Tree of Life that made me go, *Wow, Qabala is incredibly queer.*

That hidden half of the face also reminds us that Kether contains the potential for *all*; therefore, it includes the potential for all manifested and unmanifested genders, sexes, and sexualities. In that regard, Kether is the queerest of the spheres, containing the potential for queer identities we can't even conceive of. "If you manifest all of me, I shall become queerer

· · · · · · · · · · · · · ·
55. Penczak, *The Temple of High Witchcraft*, 466.

than you can possibly imagine," says Obi-Wan Kether. It is all genders, all sexualities, all sexes possible: the ultimate omnigender, omnisexual being.

We can look at Kether from another queer perspective, though. We can see Kether as a purely agender, asexual being: Kether exists before energy and before form, before any sort of expression, and we established in the Netzach chapter that Kether, like most spheres in the Tree of Life, exists before gender or sexuality can be differentiated. Further, Kether, by itself, emanates all three pillars and all the other nine spheres: in other words, Kether reproduces asexually.

Kether is everything and all possibilities, and yet it is also the absence of any expression or identification. Frankly, I can't think of anything queerer than that.

At the top of the Queer Community Triangle, Kether reminds us of that which binds the queer community together: our *queerness*. In the introduction, I said I use the word *queer* because it's an umbrella big enough to contain all the identities recognized in the LGBTQIAP2S acronym as well as non-cisheteronormative identities that aren't included in that acronym or haven't yet been identified. Kether, representing all existing and potential sexualities and genders, brings us together for our common cause.

Queer community is important. Our connections to each other are important. Together, we can make the world a better place for everyone, not just those in our community. The more people who have civil rights, the more everyone benefits. There's room under the umbrella for subdivided safe spaces for people when needed, but at the end of the day, we must stand together to fight with and for each other, and for the generations who will follow us.

Pathworking to Experience Kether

You may record this pathworking and play it back for yourself, have a friend read it, or read it and then walk through it based on

your memory. I recommend keeping a journal and pen or record-
ing device nearby so you can write about, draw, or record yourself
speaking about your experience immediately after you complete the
pathworking. Remember that you are in control of what happens
here, and you may end up diverting course from what I've written.
It's okay to do so!

Sit comfortably in a place where you will not be disturbed for the next fifteen minutes.

Close your eyes. Take three deep breaths, slowly, in and out. With each exhalation, let go of any tension you find in your body.

Without opening your eyes, visualize the room around you. Now picture it filling with a gray mist, starting at the floor and working its way up to the ceiling until the only thing you can see is grayness. As the mist dissipates, you find yourself in a field sitting on a small wooden platform colored olive, citrine, russet, and black. The sun is high overhead, and you feel the heat as you smell summer grasses and listen to the insects. You are conscious of, but cannot see, the gas giant Neptune far in the distance in the sky above.

As you gaze around the field, the shadow of the moon passes over the sun. The platform beneath you begins to rise straight in the air toward the sun occluded by the moon. You race upward, feeling the platform firmly beneath you, knowing you are not in danger of falling. You see a dark ring in the sky above you and you pass through it, and the moon seems to jump much closer in your sight after you do. You zoom closer and closer to the moon, and then suddenly it seems you pass through it, and the sun is blindingly bright on your face and fiercely hot until you pass through it as well, and you soar through space toward a brilliant blue planet: Neptune. You get closer and closer … and suddenly you begin to slow down, and you feel as though you are fading out of sync with your body. Your vision becomes fuzzy and distorted. You hear ambient, distorted sounds and you feel as though you are passing through a thick membrane. And then, just as suddenly, the sensation stops, and you continue to hurtle toward Neptune. Once the planet fills your view, you are surrounded by a dazzling, bright mist that seems like it's made of diamond dust.

You wait for the glittering mist to dissipate, but ... it doesn't. You feel your senses expand, you feel your edges become diffuse, and you feel pieces of yourself dissolve into the glittery mist.

(Pause.)

The mist—and you—begin to coalesce, all the pieces pulling together, condensing, getting tighter and denser, until everything becomes a single, bright, impossibly tiny dot in a dark void. There is no sound. There is no sensation.

All is one.

The entire Tree is there, but it is inert.

There is no breath.

There is no heartbeat.

There is no movement.

Nothing exists.

All is potential, and it is overwhelming how much there *is* that *is not* in this place that is not a place, this time that is not a time.

You are zero. You are the pause before the breath. You are the DNA of the universe. You are the moment before the spark, the moment before the big bang.

(Pause.)

Boom.

You can feel yourself expand, becoming pure energy, every piece of you flying out in a different direction, swirling and rushing.

Then you feel that energy forming into a pattern, something resembling you.

You become aware of time passing. You can see all three dimensions of the shape of yourself forming. You become aware of your potential, the things you could become.

You become aware of your limitations, of the things that hold you back.

You have a moment of feeling perfectly in balance, an equilibrium between your potential and your limits that is your ideal self.

You are suddenly filled with passion, with momentum, with primal energy.

You are suddenly filled with knowledge, and you remember your name.

You remember that all this is happening within your imagination. You see the forms of many things, including the wooden platform you rode earlier.

And then you are surprised to find yourself sitting on that platform, back in the field where you began, the sun bright overhead, the sounds of small animals and insects in the air, the smell of fresh greenery abounding. You feel yourself firm on the earth.

Take a moment to appreciate that which you feel, that which you see, that which you hear.

Eventually, the air around you fills with a pearly gray mist until you can no longer see the field. When the mist dissipates, you find yourself seated comfortably once more. Take a deep breath, wiggle your fingers and your toes, and when you are ready, open your eyes. If you have any thoughts or impressions from this pathworking you wish to remember, write or draw them in your journal, or record yourself speaking about them while they're still fresh in your mind.

Bringing It All Together

Kether is the sphere of ultimate unity and ultimate potential. It's a blueprint of everything that could be, though not necessarily everything that will be, which means it contains patterns for genders and sexualities we can't even imagine. In this way, it's the queerest sphere imaginable. Kether reminds us of that which binds us together, as its energy is contained in every path and sphere of the Tree. It is the source of all things.

While it may seem blissful to remain in a state of inert unity, we must remember we live in Malkuth and have things to do! The next part of this book will offer some great options for ways you can work with the Tree of Life in your magick.

PART 3

Qabala Workings

Qabala isn't just a philosophy or a lens to view the universe: it's a tool you can use in your magick. I've developed several workings that may be particularly helpful to queer magickal practitioners, but I think just about everyone can find something useful in the pages that follow.

As you approach these workings, please be conscious to obtain your materials from ethical sources as much as possible. There are some excellent brick-and-mortar shops and online shops that specialize in ethically sourced crystals, incense, herbs, and more. Further, feel free to substitute materials and tweak instructions based on your budget, availability of materials, and personal practice style. The power of your intent matters more than having any particular physical object I recommend for a working. The working should make sense to *you*.

Manifesting Big Change:
Get that Job, Finish that Project

This working uses candles representing the full Tree of Life to draw down energy into manifesting something big in your life. This is a working I've successfully used to get a job I really wanted and to get this book written! It does take quite a bit of time, though, and is most effective if it can stay set up in one place for several weeks or months. If you don't have a permanent space to set this up, you may try creating Qabala meditation beads instead (see working on page 199), which is a highly portable working with a similar purpose.

Supplies:

- A small broom, or sacred smoke used for energetic cleansing, such as frankincense incense or resin

- 9 unscented, tall jar candles, one for each sphere except Malkuth, in their corresponding colors (white, gray, black, blue, red, yellow, green, orange, purple). Dollar stores and grocery stores are great places to get these candles inexpensively—they are often sold as prayer candles. Using jar candles as opposed to tapers will keep your altar clean from wax drips, and they are generally safer.

- A pentacle, offering plate, or bowl: note that this working may take several months, so use a tool or dish you won't need to use for other purposes during that time.

- Altar cloth or cloths, preferably in at least one of Malkuth's colors: citrine, russet, olive, or black

- A surface that will be big enough to hold all the candles (at least 1.5 × 2.5 feet) and won't need to be regularly cleaned or disturbed

- Piece of paper and a pen

- A crystal, preferably amethyst, citrine, or quartz

- A stick lighter or long matches that can reach inside the tall jar candles

Time: A few weeks or months, depending on what you're trying to do

Setup:

Energetically cleanse the space you will be using as an altar during this working. Use a small broom and visualize sweeping away any unwanted energy from the space, or use cleansing smoke.

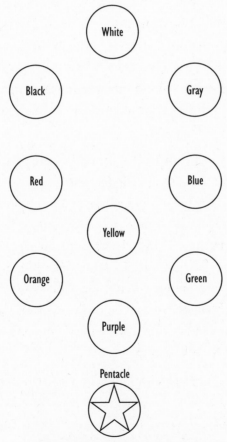

Figure 25: Candle and pentacle
or offering plate/bowl arrangement

Place the altar cloth, then lay out the candles like the Tree of Life on top of it. Put the pentacle, offering plate, or bowl in Malkuth's place.

Ground and center yourself with some deep breaths. If it is part of your practice and you wish to do so, cast sacred space around yourself and the altar, and invite your preferred protective deities or spirits to watch over you.

Spend time envisioning, as clearly as possible, what you *really* want. Try not to focus on specific situations or people so much as outcomes. Rather than focusing on a specific job or relationship you want, for example, think about how you want to feel and be treated in your desired scenario. Sometimes things that look awesome actually aren't, after all. I've worked really hard to get jobs I desperately wanted only to get rejected … and found out months later that they were deeply toxic work environments, and it was a good thing I didn't end up there.

Once you have your desire in mind, write it down on the paper in ink. Be sure to include some detail, but don't be so specific that the magick doesn't have room to do its work, or that you end up in an undesirable situation. For example, instead of writing "I want an account manager position at XYZ company by next week," write something like, "I want my next job to be one where I feel valued and can use my skills to their fullest, where I enjoy my work and my coworkers, and where I am paid a wage that allows me to afford all my bills with extra to save."

Once you're satisfied with how it's written, fold the paper so it fits neatly on or in your pentacle, plate, or bowl, and place it there. Charge the crystal with your intent, and place the crystal on top of the paper.

The Work:

Ground and center yourself. Breathe deeply. Focus your mind on your desired outcome written on the paper. Visualize it as clearly as you can. Imagine how you'll feel when it's true. Read your writing out loud, especially the first few times you do this.

Then, light the candles in order, following the Lightning Flash, saying the name of each as you light it:

1. "Kether"—white candle

2. "Chokmah"—gray candle

3. "Binah"—black candle

4. "Chesed"—blue candle

6. "Geburah"—red candle

7. "Tiphareth"—yellow candle

8. "Netzach"—green candle

9. "Hod"—orange candle

10. "Yesod"—purple candle

Once the candles are lit, trace your finger in the air above them, starting just above Kether, visualizing a bright light emanating from your finger as you draw the Lightning Flash three times over the candles in sequence, ending at the pentacle, offering plate, or bowl as you say the following:

From beyond the veils, into Kether, Chokmah, Binah, Chesed, Geburah, Tiphareth, Netzach, Hod, Yesod, into manifestation

… into manifestation

… into manifestation

This is my Will. [Hold your hand over the pentacle, offering plate, or bowl.]

If you wish, add, *"So mote it be," "And so it is,"* or whatever wording works for you in your practice.

Leave the candles burning as long as you're able—I suggest thirty to sixty minutes.

Extinguish the candles in the same order they were lit, from Kether back down to Malkuth.

Each time you extinguish a candle, visualize energy flowing down the Lightning Flash. Then, when they are all out, say:

Though the flames are extinguished, the magick still flows. This working continues.

Do this working every day for a week, then at least once a week after that for as long as it takes to bring your goal into manifestation. If any candle burns all the way down before your desire is manifested, replace it with a candle of the same type and color. The new candles will become consecrated as you repeat the working each week.

When the working is complete, save the candles and use them for future Qabala workings. When they're fully burned down, recycle the jars.

As with all magick, the work you do in the mundane world needs to support this working. You won't get that job if you don't apply or if your resume is hastily thrown together, for example. Work to keep the flow of energy going in the right direction with your mundane actions.

Chosen Name Ritual

If you decide to change your name, this ritual will help the new name stick to you by making it resonate with the Tree of Life within. I encourage you to customize this ritual, adding components that are part of your regular ritual practice, removing parts that don't feel right to you, and doing whatever feels right in the moment. If deities are not part of your practice, simply eliminate the mentions of them. Many thanks to Robin Fennelly, who contributed many components of this ritual.

Supplies:

- A marker, or a graphic design program and a printer

- A piece of cardstock

- Glitter and other craft supplies (optional)

- A small broom, or sacred smoke used for energetic cleansing, such as frankincense incense or resin

- A small table or altar

- An altar cloth of your choosing

- A pen

- A new, blank journal

- A new candle in a color that resonates with you and your new name, and a candle holder if needed. You'll want a candle big enough that you can light it several times before it burns down all the way.

- Lighter or matches

Time: An hour, plus time to design the sigil

Setup:

Spend some time creating a sigil with the letters of your new name. Play with rotating the letters, overlapping them, and connecting them in different ways until you have something that feels right. Feel free to incorporate other symbols that are meaningful to your transformation into the sigil, but don't overcomplicate it too much.

Draw or print the final sigil on the cardstock and cut around the edges of it. Add glitter or any embellishments you wish.

The Work:

Ground and center yourself. Cleanse your ritual space with the broom or sacred smoke.

Put the altar cloth on the small table or altar. Place your sigil, pen, journal, candle, and lighter or matches on the table or altar.

Cast sacred space if that is part of your practice. Call in your patron deities and spirits as desired.

Read the statement of intent:

On this day of [date], I honor my birth/previous name, [old name]. I leave this name behind with love and gratitude for the ways it has served and supported me. I hold this name as memory of who I was. In the beauty and truth of rebirth, growth, and transformation, I will claim the mantle of who I have become. In witness of the seen and unseen, I step into my power by today claiming a new name: [new name].

Light your candle.

Hold up the journal and say:

I dedicate this journal of naming that it may hold the words, wisdom, and vibration of who I am and how I am named in all of the worlds. May it know my names. May it know me.

If you wish, add, *"So mote it be," "And so it is,"* or whatever wording seems natural to you in your practice.

Take up your sigil and say:

I call to the vibration and energetic signature of this, my name—[new name]—that it may resonate and echo throughout all levels of my being in all of the worlds.

Hold the sigil close to you and awaken all of your chakras or parts of self in whatever manner you are accustomed. As you go through each chakra or part of self, after awakening, make the declaration:

I awaken my [chakra or part of self] that you may know me as [new name] in all of the worlds and in all parts of my being.

Open the journal. On the first page, write: *I am [new name].*

On the second page, write: *I am [new name].* Below that, draw the Mercury symbol:

Write below that: *By the naming and communication powers of Hod and Mercury, I declare this to be my true name.*

On the third page, write: *I am [new name].* Below that, draw the Venus symbol:

Write below that: *With the victory of Netzach and Venus, and with the power of love, I declare this to be my true name.*

On the fourth page, write: *I am [new name].* Below that, draw the Mars symbol:

Write below that: *With the courage of Geburah and Mars, I declare this to be my true name.*

On the fifth page, write: *I am [new name].* Below that, draw the Jupiter symbol:

Write below that: *With the visionary powers of Chesed and Jupiter, I declare this to be my true name.*

On the sixth page, write: *I am [new name].* Below that, draw a crescent moon:

Write below that: *With the powers of Yesod, the moon, my unconscious mind, and the powers of my own birth and death, I declare this to be my true name.*

On the seventh page, write: *I am [new name].* Below that, draw the sun symbol:

Write below that: *With the bright, shining, healing powers of the sun and all the healing deities and spirits, I declare this to be my true name.*

On the eighth page, write: *I am [new name].* Below that, draw the Malkuth symbol:

Write below that: *By the powers of Malkuth and manifestation on this plane, I declare this to be my true name.*

Spend some time meditating, communing with your deities and spirits, and seeing what messages come to you. When you are finished meditating, open your journal and write any thoughts or observations starting on the ninth page.

When you are ready, thank your deities and spirits and open the sacred space you have created in whatever manner is part of your practice.

If it is safe to do so, leave your altar up with the candle lit for a few hours, or move the candle to another location to continue to burn for an hour or so. Light it whenever you have feelings of uncertainty, impostor syndrome, or hardship around your name change. When it is fully burned down, dispose of what remains in a sacred fire, if possible.

Chokmah: Reinvigoration

Need some energy? This meditation will give you a quick burst of Chokmah's effervescent energy and build your connection with Chokmah when done repeatedly over time.

Supplies:
- A piece of paper with a gray-colored circle and the symbol for Uranus drawn onto it (optional)

Time: At least 5 minutes

Setup: None

The Work:

Find a place you can sit comfortably for a few minutes. Ground and center yourself. If it is part of your practice, cast sacred space around yourself and invite your preferred protective deities or spirits to watch over you.

Breathe deeply and slowly. Visualize a gray circle with the symbol for Uranus overlaid atop it. (Or, if you prefer, gaze at a physical one you have drawn.) Focus.

When you are ready, close your eyes and feel yourself fall into that circle, and feel yourself surrounded by effervescent energy, swirling and shooting out in all directions. Feel yourself begin to dissolve into that energy, joining with it, riding the excited waves and bursts. Enjoy this sensation for as long as you like.

Eventually, imagine the energy begin to coalesce again into *you.* Feel every cell within you vibrate, alive and excited. Feel yourself detach from the gray circle, see it fall away from your sight. When you are ready, open your eyes.

If you cast sacred space, open it at this time and thank your deities and helping spirits.

If you created a tangible gray circle, feel free to hang on to it for future meditations. If you wish to dispose of it, do so in sacred fire if possible.

Chesed Leadership Charm

Chesed is a potent sphere for working with the powers of expansion and vision—both qualities needed in a leader. If you're being called to take up the mantle of leadership in your job, community group, or spiritual group, yet you're unsure of your capabilities, working with Chesed can help charge you up and set you on the best course for success. This working creates a Chesed-powered charm to bring you confidence in your leadership abilities.

Supplies:

- A small broom, or sacred smoke used for energetic cleansing, such as frankincense incense or resin

- A square blue cloth

- A small, royal blue candle and candleholder

- A match or lighter

- A blue stone, or a piece of jewelry with one or many blue stones

- A piece of paper with the Jupiter sigil drawn on it (if you don't know the planetary sigils by heart)

- Cedar incense

- Incense holder or censer

- A bell, chime, or singing bowl

Time: 10+ minutes

Setup:

Consider doing this working on a Thursday, the day aligned with Jupiter, the planet associated with Chesed. For extra oomph, choose your working time to be during one of Jupiter's planetary hours on the day you're doing the working. Planetary hours vary by day, based on sunrise and sunset. Look for a planetary hours calculator online or in your phone's app store to find when Jupiter's planetary hours are on your chosen day.

Energetically cleanse the space you will be using as an altar during this working. Use a small broom and visualize sweeping away any unwanted energy from the space, or use cleansing smoke—whichever aligns with your practice.

Set up an altar space with the cloth, the candle, the stone or jewelry item, the Jupiter sigil (if needed), the incense, the incense holder or censer, the lighter, and the bell, chime, or singing bowl.

The Work:

Ground and center yourself. Focus on your breath for a few full breath cycles. If it is part of your practice, cast sacred space around yourself and the altar, and invite your preferred protective deities or spirits to watch over you.

Light the candle.

Visualize the blue sphere of Chesed overlaid atop your altar. Hold your hand over the stone or jewelry item, and allow energy to flow from that sphere, through you, into the object.

Say, either out loud or to yourself, "I call upon the powers of Chesed, the powers of vision and expansion, to empower this object, that I may step confidently into my leadership capabilities without hesitation."

Draw the Jupiter sigil in the air over the stone or jewelry item. Visualize it sinking into the object. Visualize the blue sphere of Chesed sinking into the object.

Ring the bell, chime, or singing bowl four times. Each time it rings, visualize the sound waves flowing into the object.

Say, "This working is done." If you wish, add, "So mote it be," "And so it is," or whatever wording works for you in your practice. Extinguish the candle. If you cast sacred space, open it at this time.

Keep the stone with you or wear the jewelry item, particularly at times when you are called upon to act in a leadership role.

You may recharge the object with this same ritual whenever you feel it is needed—no more frequently than monthly. Before recharging, submerge the object in salt for an hour to remove any unwanted energy that may have built up around it. Feel free to reuse and replace the candle as needed. Any remnants should be disposed of in sacred fire, if possible.

Geburah: Letting Go

The power of Geburah helps us to release that which no longer serves, that which holds us back. Geburah digests and removes harmful things from our lives, but first we must acknowledge that we need to be rid of those things. If you feel like something isn't right but you can't figure out what exactly, this ritual will help you identify it.

Supplies:

- A small red candle and candleholder

- A match or lighter

- A journal and pen, or recording device

Time: 20+ minutes

Setup:

If moon magick is part of your practice, do this working during the waning or dark moon.

Prepare a place where you can meditate quietly for twenty minutes or so. If needed, use headphones and a white noise app or ambient music to help you focus and avoid distractions.

The Work:

> Ground and center yourself. If it is part of your practice, cast sacred space around yourself, and invite your preferred protective deities or spirits to watch over you.
>
> Light the candle and stare at the flame. Watch it dance. Breathe.
>
> Now keep visualizing the flame as you close your eyes and turn your focus inward. See the flame in your mind's eye. Watch it burn and flicker.
>
> Now shape the flame into a red sphere: Geburah. Feel its intensity; feel its heat.
>
> Now fall into the sphere and see that redness become a forge. Smell the fire. Feel the smoke sting your eyes a bit. See a glowing piece of metal taken from the fire and placed onto an anvil to be hammered into shape. Watch as it becomes sharper and stronger. What is being created?
>
> As you watch, notice how tiny bits of metal fall off the metal being shaped. By losing these pieces, the metal being shaped becomes stronger.
>
> Think on what you need to release in your life to become stronger. What holds you back? What drags you down? As you watch the metal take shape, imagine that metal is you

and see what dross is shaken off as you are forged into something stronger and more *you*. What do you see?

Watch the dross collect on the ground beneath you. Scoop it into your hands and offer it love. Remember that at one time, these were things you thought you needed. Thank them. And release them into the void. Watch them slowly disappear until they wink out of existence.

See yourself surrounded by a golden glow. This is the power of Tiphareth, the place of balance. Feel yourself in greater alignment and harmony after sacrificing that which holds you back. Hear the world sing around you.

When you are ready, open your eyes. Thank the flame for its guidance. Write down or record any practical steps you need to take to remove these things from your life, and make a commitment to work toward them over the next moon cycle. If you cast sacred space, open it at this time and thank your deities and helping spirits.

If you wish and are able, allow the candle to burn all the way down as a final act of release. (Be careful: Do not leave candles unattended. It's okay to do this over the course of several days.) Dispose of any remains of the candle in sacred fire, if possible.

Qabala Meditation Beads

Malas, also called japamalas, have been in use for thousands of years, particularly in Buddhism, Hinduism, Sikhism, Jainism, and other spiritual traditions. In Sanskrit, the word mala means garland, and japa means repetition.[56] *By repeating a brief intention or mantra as you touch each individual bead on the traditional 108-bead strand, you effectively reprogram your brain.*

Though inspired by japamalas, Qabala meditation beads are different in a few ways. Most importantly, their use is different: Rather than repeating a mantra to achieve inner calm or enlightenment, you will be focusing your energy on manifesting something by working your way down the Lightning Flash or working on releasing something by working your way up the Lightning Flash. On a practical level, there are some other differences: the strand contains 104 beads instead of the traditional 108; there is no tassel, but rather a series of 4 beads at the end; and they are not worked symmetrically on both sides—the pattern of the beads must continue from Kether to Malkuth all the way around.

One of the great things about Qabala meditation beads is that they are highly portable. No need to worry about lighting candles or incense, or drawing attention to yourself in a public place—you can take a strand of beads anywhere and silently work through your repeated intention. They're a similar magickal working to the manifestation spell on page 182, but because you have to hold a very

. . . .

56. "The History, Purpose and Value of Meditation Mala Beads," Buddha Groove, accessed April 12, 2021, https://blog.buddhagroove.com/the-history-purpose-and-value-of -meditation-mala-beads/; "Japamala—The Spiritual String Of Beads," Amar Chitra Katha, March 1, 2021, https://www.amarchitrakatha.com/mythologies/japamala-the -spiritual-string-of-beads/.

clear image in your mind throughout, Qabala meditation beads may be better for smaller, simpler manifestations rather than big life changes. Your mileage may, of course, vary.

Supplies:

- A 15-foot strand of thin black or white nylon cord (I recommend Beadaholique Twisted Nylon Cord, Size 18). This seems like a lot of string, but trust me, you will need it because you'll be making a lot of knots in it.

- A pair of jeweler's tweezers: these are tweezers with a bend at the end

- Sharp sewing scissors

- A beading needle threader

- Seam sealant (such as Fray Check), or clear or black nail polish

- The following beads, each 8–12 mm in size with at least 1.5 mm holes. I recommend using semiprecious stones, preferably ones that aren't dyed, for maximum magickal oomph, but less-expensive colored glass beads will also work. Get a few extra of each bead in case a bead cracks or goes missing while you're stringing them. The quantities below are the minimum needed.

    * 14 multicolored beads for Malkuth, e.g., red creek jasper (Red creek jasper is a good choice here, as it includes olive and russet colors. Try to find stones with some blend of olive, russet, goldish color, or black.)

    * 10 purple beads for Yesod, e.g., purple amethyst

    * 10 orange beads for Hod, e.g., orange banded agate

    * 10 dark green beads for Netzach, e.g., moss agate

    * 10 golden beads for Tiphareth, e.g., citrine

    * 10 red beads for Geburah, e.g., red jasper or carnelian

* 10 royal blue beads for Chesed, e.g., azurite

* 10 black beads for Binah, e.g., onyx, lava, or jet

* 10 gray or pearly beads for Chokmah, e.g., sardonyx or moonstone

* 10 clear beads for Kether, e.g., clear quartz

Time:

Approximately 3 hours to create the beaded strand and approximately 10 minutes to do a full rotation of your focused intention

Setup:

Tie a tight, double knot in the middle of the 15-foot strand of nylon cord. This will be the back of the loop, and we'll work our way to the front by stringing beads on either side, starting with a set of 10 on one side of the center knot and proceeding to the next set of 10 on the other side. As you slide on each bead, focus on the sphere it represents, saying its name out loud if you are comfortable doing so.

You will slide beads on, one at a time, and put double knots between each bead. Ideally, you don't want the beads to wiggle—you want them to be snug up against the knots. To keep the knots tight against the beads, use a method called pearl knotting. I'll explain it here, but it may be easier to search for a video online that demonstrates it:

1. Slide your first bead (Kether) down to the center knot.

2. Tie a loose overhand knot above the bead on the open side of the string.

3. Reach *through* the loop of the overhand knot with your jeweler's tweezers. Press down on the bead to allow as little space as possible between the bead and the knot.

4. While continuing to apply pressure to the bead with the tweezers, pull the knot tight. Don't worry about the tweezers being in the

way. When you have the knot as tight as possible, simply slide your tweezers out and pull the knot tight.

5. Grasp the string with the tweezers just above your new knot, and use the tweezers to press the knot down onto the bead. That'll make it a little tighter.

6. Repeat this process to tie the second knot on top of that knot.

Continue this process, sliding a Chokmah bead after the Kether bead on the same side of the cord, followed by Binah, Chesed, Geburah, Tiphareth, Netzach, Hod, Yesod, and Malkuth—pearl knotting between each bead. I like to put a little extra space and a couple extra knots between Chesed and Binah to represent Da'ath, but do what feels natural to you.

After you've completed one set of 10, go to the other half of the string next to your Kether bead, but start by stringing Malkuth rather than Kether. Work the beads in the opposite direction: Malkuth, Yesod, Hod, Netzach, Tiphareth, Geburah, Chesed, Binah, Chokmah, Kether. That way, the beads continue in the same order throughout the strand, with Malkuth always following Kether and starting the sequence over.

Once your second set of 10 is complete, return to the first side and do another set of 10, starting with Kether as you did with the first set. After that one, return to the second side and string another set of 10 starting with Malkuth.[57]

Once you have 10 sets of 10 beads strung, you'll finish as follows:

1. Focus on the concept of manifestation.

2. Poke the tip of the needle threader through one of the four remaining Malkuth beads.

3. Thread the two trailing ends of string through the needle threader.

4. Pull the needle threader back through the bead, pulling the two strings through the bead.

. . . .

57. Instructions based on mala creation method taught by Irene Glasse of Glasse Witch Cottage. Adapted here with permission.

5. Pearl knot in the same way you've knotted between the other beads, but with both strands held together.

6. Repeat with the remaining three Malkuth beads, continuing to focus on manifestation.

After the last bead has been strung, cut the remaining cord close to the final knot. Use a dot of seam sealant (such as Fray Check) or nail polish on the cut ends, with the intention of sealing the working and ensuring they don't unravel.

The Work:

To manifest something using the meditation beads, focus your energy on that which you want to manifest. Hold it as clearly as you can in your mind and engage all your senses as you visualize it. While visualizing your desire coming into manifestation, hold the Kether bead that is closest to the four Malkuth beads, and say "Kether," then hold the Chokmah bead and say "Chokmah," continuing your way all around until you get back to the four Malkuth beads. As you progress from Kether to Malkuth, imagine your vision becoming more real, more tangible. Repeat all the way around the strand. When you get to the four Malkuth beads, hold them each in turn, and repeat the word "manifest" each time you hold one. Engage your Will with the certainty that you are creating something.

To release something using the meditation beads, focus your energy on that which you want to release. Hold it as clearly as you can in your mind, engaging all your senses. Then hold the Malkuth bead at the end of the strand, and say, "Malkuth." Do this for the next three Malkuth beads and the first Malkuth bead next to the set of four, then continue around to Yesod, saying "Yesod," and so forth, all the way around. As you progress from Malkuth to Kether, visualize the thing you want to release slowly fading away. After you say the final "Kether," reinvigorate and engage your Will around releasing that thing, saying, "I release you, I release you, I release you." If you wish, add, "So mote it be," "And so it is," or whatever wording works for you in your practice.

Handle your Qabala meditation beads with care and store them carefully. I don't recommend wearing them: they are not a fashion statement, and depending on the stones you use, you may run the risk of breaking them if you handle them too casually. Keep your beads wrapped in some kind of padding when not in use, and only use them for their intended purpose. Submerge them in salt for an hour periodically to cleanse, then make sure to rinse off all excess salt with water and pat it dry. The beads will be continually recharged every time you use them.

Tiphareth: Balancing Your Life

Tiphareth is the sphere of balance: something we could all use! Too often, lives become unbalanced, and we feel pressure on our health, relationships, families, and careers. This working will bring you to a place of balance and encourage that feeling to reverberate through the rest of your life.

Supplies:

- A beaded necklace or bracelet, or a bowl with several crystals, rocks, or several 6-sided dice in it

- A small broom, or sacred smoke used for energetic cleansing, such as frankincense incense or resin (optional)

- An altar, including a small yellow candle and candleholder, golden-colored altar cloth, a lighter or match, a chunk of citrine or other golden-colored stone, representations of the number six, or other symbols of the number six or the color gold you have available (optional)

Time: 20+ minutes, ideally daily over the course of 6 days

Setup:

Prepare a place where you can meditate quietly for twenty minutes or so. If needed, use headphones and a white noise app or ambient music to help you focus and avoid distractions.

Consider doing this working in a place or at a time that feels liminal: dawn, dusk, in a doorway, during a dark moon, near running water, etc.

Choose an intention that fits your purpose. Some examples:

- *I seek balance in my life, and that balance seeks me in return.*

- *I call on the powers of Tiphareth to bring my life into balance.*

- *I am whole, I am centered, I am balanced.*

The Work:

If you wish to create an altar for this working, do so with intention, cleansing the space first, then focusing on each of the components individually and considering their connection to Tiphareth. If you are using a candle, light it. Focus on the yellow of the candle and the yellow in the flame.

Ground and center yourself. If it is part of your practice, cast sacred space around yourself, and invite your preferred protective deities or spirits to watch over you.

Close your eyes and visualize golden light surrounding you. Breathe. This is Tiphareth, the place of balance and harmony. Perhaps you hear some harmonic music or smell things that bring you comfort. The experience is unique to you.

Pick up your beads or your bowl containing crystals, rocks, or dice. Hold each bead or rock in turn, and as you hold it, speak the intention you have chosen. Then hold the next bead or rock. (Holding an object helps keep you focused during this working.)

Repeat holding a different bead or rock and speaking the intention at least a few dozen times. Keep your mind relaxed and focused to the best of your ability. When you feel a shift or simply feel that you are done, hold yourself quietly in that space for a while, and see what messages come to you.

When you are finished, give thanks to the powers of Tiphareth and come out of your meditation. If you used a candle, extinguish it. If you cast sacred space, open it at this time.

You may reuse the candle and other materials to repeat this working, or perform other workings, as needed. When you wish to dispose of the remains of the candle, do so in sacred fire, if possible.

Remember to journal or record any thoughts or messages you received.

Yesod: Improve Your Resiliency, Flexibility, Creativity

Exploring the creative powers of Yesod, the sphere of imagination, can be beneficial when you feel yourself becoming rigid in your thinking, when you feel stuck, or when you need to increase your creative power.

Supplies:

- A small, purple candle and candleholder

- A match or lighter

- A journal and pen or recording device

- A 20+ minute playlist of music that inspires you but doesn't distract you (instrumental is best, unless you can tune out lyrics while meditating)

- Headphones, if needed

- A small snack

Time: 20+ minutes

Setup:

Set up your candle, journal and pen or recording device, music, and headphones in a space where you won't be disturbed for twenty minutes or so. Have a small snack nearby to help you ground afterward.

The Work:

Ground and center yourself. Breathe. Focus on your breath for three full cycles. If it's part of your practice, cast sacred space around yourself, and invite your preferred protective deities or spirits to watch over you.

Put on your music (and, if needed, your headphones). Ensure it's playing loud enough to be heard, but not so loud that it's distracting.

Light your candle. Visualize the purple sphere of Yesod surrounding it, charging the flame. Study the flame. Watch it dance and glow. Breathe.

Close your eyes. Visualize a swirling, purple sphere over your third eye (the middle of your forehead). Feel it grow denser, more tangible. Now push your consciousness through it and feel yourself sail through darkness. Visualize a soft purple light in the distance, and watch it get larger in your sight until you see it become a purple-tinted window. Push yourself through the window and find yourself in a place that lives within your imagination. This place will look different to everyone. Note the details that stand out to you.

Feel yourself in this space. What can you do here? Can you stretch or contort your body in ways you can't normally? Do you have a body at all? Has your body changed form? Can you jump super high in the air? Can you fly? What does it feel like? Your only limits are your imagination.

Spend some time exploring this space. Perhaps you will meet another being or spirit. If you do, listen to what they have to tell you.

When you feel like your work is finished, find a token to bring back with you, something that reminds you of the creative fullness of Yesod. Perhaps it's a flower or a stone or something else entirely. Put the item over your heart and feel this item being absorbed within yourself—a reminder of your connection to the divine, to the infinite, to the flexible, to the source of creativity and imagination. This is part of you.

Find your way back to the purple-tinted window, and push yourself back through it. See yourself fall back through the darkness and into the swirling purple sphere over your third eye. Feel yourself slowly begin to reintegrate with your body. Wiggle your fingers and your toes.

When you are ready, open your eyes. Thank the powers of Yesod, and extinguish your candle. If you cast sacred space, open it at this time. Journal or record your experiences while they're fresh in your mind. Eat your snack and feel yourself in this body, in this place, here and now.

You may reuse the candle to repeat this working or other workings in the future. When you wish to dispose of its remains, do so in sacred fire, if possible.

The Middle Pillar:
Exploring Your Nonbinary Identity

Nonbinary people sometimes struggle with our gender identities. It can be tricky to explain how you feel, especially if you don't have a solid grasp on what you feel in the first place. For many of us, this is nebulous, new territory, and it can be scary. There aren't a lot of guidebooks or examples for how to live outside the gender binary at the time I'm writing this.

This working is a meditation practice to help you explore your identity and tune in to yourself using the Nonbinary Pillar and candles that correspond with its spheres and the nonbinary pride flag.

Supplies:

- A small broom, or sacred smoke for energetic cleansing, such as frankincense incense or resin

- 1 small, white candle to represent Kether

- 1 small, yellow candle to represent Tiphareth

- 1 small, purple candle to represent Yesod

- 1 small, black candle to represent Malkuth

- 4 candleholders for the small candles

- Matches or lighter

Time: 10–20 minutes

Setup:

Energetically cleanse your space in a manner of your choosing.

Arrange your candles on a stable surface in a line: white, then yellow, then purple, then black, with the white one furthest and the black one closest to you. Be sure you have a quiet place where you can meditate and where the candles won't be disturbed while they're lit.

The Work:

> Ground and center yourself. If it is part of your practice, cast sacred space around yourself, and invite your preferred protective deities or spirits to watch over you.
>
> Light each of your candles, saying the name of the Middle Pillar sphere each represents. Black is Malkuth, purple is Yesod, yellow is Tiphareth, and white is Kether.

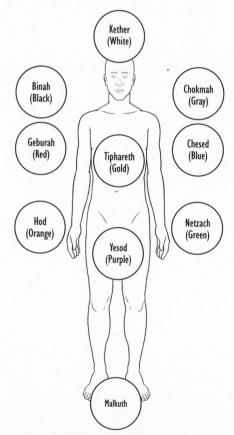

Figure 26: The spheres and the body

Gaze at the Malkuth candle. Watch the flame. Feel the floor beneath you, feel yourself embodied. Breathe.

After a minute or so, close your eyes. Hold the image of the candles in your mind. Breathe.

Become aware of your imagination, of the part of you that can visualize and sense things that are not in the physical realm. Fill your vision with the color purple. After a moment, let that color fade away, and imagine yourself staring in a mirror. As you gaze at your reflection, you see the Tree of Life glyph overlaid on top of yourself. Malkuth is at your feet. Yesod, purple, is at your hips. Hod and Netzach, orange and green, are on either side of your waist. Tiphareth, gold, is at your heart. Geburah and Chesed, red and blue, are on either side of your shoulders. Binah and Chokmah, black and gray, are on either side of your head. Kether, white, floats just above your head.

You can feel yourself balanced on that middle pillar and feel the push and pull of the energies on either side. No sphere is stronger than any other, however—you are balanced. You exist between the outside pillars. Though you can feel the energy currents throughout the Tree of Life, you hold your own place.

Ask, either out loud or to yourself: "How can I express my true gender identity in the physical realm in a way that feels right to me?"

Now look at your physical form in the mirror. Does it look like you do in the physical realm, or does your reflection look different? Pay attention to details. Is your hair different? Are your nails painted? Are you wearing any particular clothing or jewelry? Is what you're wearing colorful or monochrome? Do you have any piercings or tattoos? Study the image of yourself and ask: Does this image feel right? Does it feel natural?

If it doesn't feel right, begin visualizing adjustments. Try on different clothes. Try different hairstyles. Don't worry if it's something you've never tried before or doesn't make sense. Have fun! Play! If you don't find anything that seems right, don't worry—you can repeat this exercise whenever you need to, and ideas may come to you in dreams as well.

Say, either out loud or to yourself: "Does this mirror wish to show me anything else I should know about my identity?" Wait and see what happens.

Feel yourself balanced. See a golden glow emanate from you: the blessing of Tiphareth. Ask the mirror: "What can I do to stay in balance, to be in harmony with my true self?" Wait and see what happens.

Feel the divine spark within you, your connection with your higher self. Ask the mirror: "Does my higher self have any messages for me?" Wait and see what happens.

When you have finished, thank the mirror. Let your vision fill with purple again, and then let it dissipate. Wiggle your fingers and your toes. Take a deep breath. Open your eyes and blow out the candles. If you cast sacred space, open it at this time and thank your deities and helping spirits.

You may reuse the candles for other Qabala workings. If you wish to dispose of them, do so in sacred fire, if possible.

Create Your Own Tree

You're probably tired of this phrase by now, but I'll say it again: Every generation of Qabalists has the obligation and the opportunity to add to the treasury of knowledge and understanding of the Tree of Life. In order to do that, you must understand the Tree in a way that makes sense to you. The best way to approach this is to make your own Tree.

The first Tree of Life I created was to help me better understand and visualize the correspondences between the tarot, astrology, and Qabala. I used a graphic design program and mocked up the Tree, colored the circles, and then put the corresponding tarot cards and astrological symbols on the various paths and spheres. I then printed it on a five-by-three-foot poster, and as I worked with the Tree of Life, I wrote stuff on sticky notes and stuck them on the related spheres/paths. All of that is still on my wall, and I still refer to it regularly as I work with the Tree.

The second Tree of Life I created was a Steven Universe Qabala! I was slightly obsessed with the show at the time and kept thinking about how various characters aligned with the spheres.

Later, while writing a queer Qabala series for my blog, I created a Tree of Life out of the images I used for each post.

Putting the Tree of Life into terms I understood, into a framework that was my own, helped me deepen my relationship with the Tree. I highly recommend this activity for anyone who wants to continue their Qabala study.

Supplies:
- Notebook (graph paper may be easiest)
- Pencil or pen

Time: Not fixed

Setup: None

The Work:

Referencing the Tree of Life glyph on the next page, draw or trace the glyph on a piece of paper.

If it's helpful, include the sphere names and add keywords near the spheres to help you remember their meanings and correspondences.

Spend some time thinking of what the Tree and the individual spheres mean to you. Add notes, colors, and designs to the Tree as you see fit. Don't overthink it—do what feels natural. Feel free to use a graphic design program to build the Tree as you finalize your ideas, if that's something you'd like to do.

If you've got a particular favorite TV show, movie, book, or video game, think how those characters might fit in with the Tree of Life. Even if you can't think of something to align with every sphere, it's still worth the effort! Hint: Action, adventure, and fantasy films and shows with lots of characters tend to work particularly well here, as they often lean on classic archetypes.

If you're an herbalist or like working with crystals, think about which herbs or stones would align with each sphere and why. (There are traditional alignments for each, and they're worth studying, but your own interpretation is also valid!)

I recommend working on this over a period of a few days or weeks. Come back to it; see if your ideas have changed or shifted or if you have more to add.

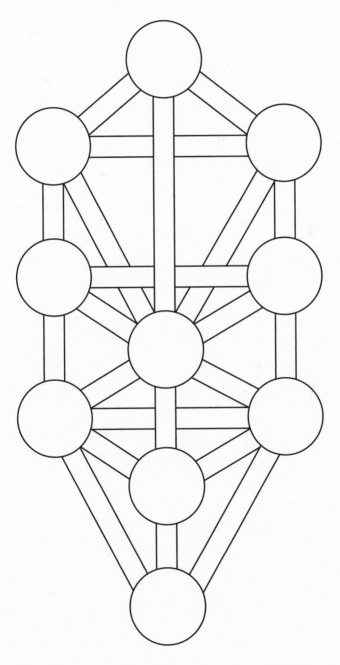

CONCLUSION

I specifically called this book *Queer Qabala* rather than *Queering the Qabala* because the more I looked at Qabala through the lens of queerness, the more I realized that queerness isn't just a lens. Qabala is, at its core, fundamentally queer. Representations of nonbinary and fluid gender and sexuality can be found throughout the Tree of Life, and you don't even need to look hard to find them.

I don't need to queer the Tree of Life because the Tree simply *is* queer. I wanted to show it to you without all the unnecessary trappings generations of patriarchy have hung upon its branches, and my hope is that through this book, I have done so. The Tree has *so much potential* as a powerful and queer magickal tool.

If you came to this book as an experienced Qabalist, my hope is that I've given you some food for thought. If you teach and write about Qabala, I hope you will consider the queerness of the Tree of Life and incorporate some of these ideas into your teachings, if you haven't already. If you have queer students interested in Qabala—inevitably, you do—I hope you will recommend this book to them so they don't have to take the long, windy road I took to get to this point.

If you came to this book as a Qabala newbie, my hope is that I've given you a good introduction to the Tree of Life, made you hungry to learn more, and inspired you to use it in your regular practice. I hope I've demonstrated that the Qabala is both super queer and incredibly powerful, and I hope you have found the suggested workings to be both useful and potent. The further reading section on the next page has a list of recommended next books to read, and I hope you'll consider them.

Many times in this book, I said that it's incumbent upon every generation of Qabalists to deepen and add to our collective understanding of the Tree of Life. Our forebears' understanding of the Tree was incomplete and colored by the lens of their time and societal understanding—as is ours, of course! After reading this book, I hope you feel called to take up this charge, to create your own Tree of Life (see page 213), and to tell other magickal practitioners how you see the Tree and how you use it in your magickal work and daily life. Your perspective is both unique and valuable.

Even more than that, though, I hope this book can be a springboard for others to write more about queer Qabala, to take these ideas deeper and further than this introductory book had the space to accomplish. A book is, after all, created and published at a fixed point in time, whereas our world and our understanding of it are constantly evolving. Our study of Qabala must, likewise, continue to grow and change with time. May this book be one of many collective steps toward a future of more inclusive and expansive Qabala and other magickal studies.

FURTHER READING

The following books will benefit your study of Qabala or queerness in magick. No book is perfect or free of problematic language—including the one you're reading now, as language is ever-evolving, and I certainly have my own blind spots. I encourage you to read with an open mind and open heart, particularly when approaching the much older Qabala books.

Intro to Qabala

Five books that I'm going to recommend as next reads after this book are more modern and less-problematic works. They are well-written, well-edited, and easy to follow. Each of these books gives you a good way to begin to understand the basics of Qabala without too much frustration.

- *Qabalah for Wiccans: Ceremonial Magic on the Pagan Path* by Jack Chanek (2021)

- *The Temple of High Witchcraft: Ceremonies, Spheres, and the Witches' Qabalah* by Christopher Penczak (2007)

- *The Witches Qabala: The Pagan Path and the Tree of Life* by Ellen Cannon Reed (1997)

- *The Kabbalah Tree: A Journey of Balance & Growth* by Rachel Pollack (2004)

- *Falling Through the Tree of Life: Embodied Kabbalah* by Jane Meredith (2022)

The More-Problematic Classics

Once you're through those books, it's a good idea to work through some of the classics in Hermetic Qabala study. Though these books can be painful at times, they do contain a lot of helpful information and different ways to think about the spheres and paths. Approach these books with the awareness that you will need to do some extra mental labor to glean the valuable bits while either ignoring or picking apart some of the binary, homophobic, ableist, sexist, or racist stuff you'll find. Take their more antiquated beliefs with several grains of salt, maybe write a few curse words in the margins, and then focus your attention on the more valuable information contained within.

- *The Mystical Qabalah* by Dion Fortune (originally published in 1935)

- *A Practical Guide to Qabalistic Symbolism* by Gareth Knight (originally published in 1965)

- *A Garden of Pomegranates: An Outline of the Qabalah* by Israel Regardie (originally published in 1932)

Tarot and Qabala

If you're into tarot, I recommend this book as well:

- *Tarot and the Tree of Life: Finding Everyday Wisdom in the Minor Arcana* by Isabel Radow Kliegman (1997)

Queer Magick

For books on queerness and magick in general, I highly recommend:

- *Outside the Charmed Circle: Exploring Gender & Sexuality in Magical Practice* by Misha Magdalene (2020)

- *Queering Your Craft: Witchcraft from the Margins* by Cassandra Snow (2020)

- *Queer Magic: Power Beyond Boundaries,* edited by Lee Harrington and Tai Fenix Kulystin (2018)

- *All Acts of Love & Pleasure: Inclusive Wicca* by Yvonne Aburrow (2014)

APPENDIX

Pronunciation Guide

This pronunciation guide contains one way to pronounce these names, but it's not definitive. The names of the spheres are transliterated into Roman letters from Hebrew. There are also many different variants of Hebrew, both ancient and modern, and each have their own way to say these names. As such, spellings and pronunciation tend to vary across resources and practitioners.

Qabala: kah-BAH-lah or kah-bah-LAH

Malkuth: Mal-KOOTH

Yesod: Yeh-SOD

Hod: Hahd

Netzach: NET-zack or NET-zach, with a gutteral "ch" sound

Tiphareth: TIH-far-eth

Geburah: GEH-bur-ah, with the "b" very soft, almost like a "v" sound

Chesed: HEH-sehd or CHEH-sehd, with a gutteral "ch" sound

Binah: BIH-nah

Chokmah: HOCK-mah or CHOK-mah, with a
gutteral "ch" sound

Kether: KEHT-her[58]

---

58. Adapted from Reed, *The Witches Qabala*, 183–84.

BIBLIOGRAPHY

Aburrow, Yvonne. "Inclusive Wicca Manifesto." In *Queer Magic: Power Beyond Boundaries*, edited by Lee Harrington and Tai Fenix Kulystin, 7–14. Anchorage: Mystic Productions Press, 2018.

Adams, Douglas. *The Hitchhiker's Guide to the Galaxy*. New York: Harmony Books, 2000.

Allen, Lasara Firefox. *Jailbreaking the Goddess: A Radical Revisioning of Feminist Spirituality*. Woodbury, MN: Llewellyn Publications, 2016.

Ashcroft-Nowicki, Dolores. *The Shining Paths: An Experiential Journey Through the Tree of Life*. Loughborough, UK: Thoth Publications, 2006.

Barkataki, Susanna. "Mālā Beads & Their Proper Use." Updated November 12, 2020. https://www.susannabarkataki.com/post/mala-beads -their-proper-use.

Barker, Meg-John, and Jules Scheele. *Gender: A Graphic Guide*. London: Icon Books Ltd., 2020.

———. *Queer: A Graphic History*. London: Icon Books Ltd., 2016.

———. *Sexuality: A Graphic Guide*. London: Icon Books Ltd., 2021.

Bornstein, Kate. *My New Gender Workbook: A Step-by-Step Guide to Achieving World Peace Through Gender Anarchy and Sex Positivity.* New York: Routledge, 2013.

Bowie, David, and Jennifer Connelly. *Labyrinth.* Directed by Jim Henson. LucasFilm: 2018.

Dominguez Jr., Ivo, *Keys to Perception: A Practical Guide to Psychic Development.* York Beach, ME: Weiser, 2017.

———. *Practical Astrology for Witches and Pagans: Using the Planets and the Stars for Effective Spellwork, Rituals, and Magickal Work.* San Francisco: Weiser, 2016.

———. "Redefining and Repurposing Polarity." In *Queer Magic: Power Beyond Boundaries,* edited by Lee Harrington and Tai Fenix Kulystin, 174–79. Anchorage: Mystic Productions Press, 2018.

DuQuette, Lon Milo. *The Chicken Qabalah of Rabbi Lamed Ben Clifford: A Dilettante's Guide to What You Do and* Do Not *Need to Know to Become a Qabalist.* York Beach, ME: Weiser, 2001.

Fennelly, Robin. *The Inner Chamber, Volume 2: Poetry of the Spheres, Qabala.* Philadelphia: Robin Fennelly, 2012.

Forge, Thumper. "Cancelled for Renovations: More Thoughts on Closed Practices." *Fivefold Law* (blog). Patheos. May 19, 2021. https://www.patheos.com/blogs/fivefoldlaw/2021/05/19/cancelled-for-renovations-more-thoughts-on-closed-practices/.

———. "Over the Moon (or, an Open/Shut Case of Open/Closed Practice)." *Fivefold Law* (blog). Patheos. February 19, 2021. https://www.patheos.com/blogs/fivefoldlaw/2021/02/19/over-the-moon-or-an-open-shut-case-of-open-closed-practice/.

Fortune, Dion. *The Mystical Qabalah.* San Francisco: Weiser, 1998. Kindle.

Gibran, Kahlil. "On Joy and Sorrow." Poets.org. Academy of American Poets. Accessed April 11, 2021. https://poets.org/poem/joy-and -sorrow.

Harrington, Lee, and Tai Fenix Kulystin, eds. *Queer Magic: Power Beyond Boundaries.* Anchorage: Mystic Productions Press, 2018.

"Hermaphroditos." Theoi Project. Accessed May 14, 2021. https://www .theoi.com/Ouranios/ErosHermaphroditos.html.

"The History, Purpose and Value of Meditation Mala Beads." Buddha Groove. Accessed April 12, 2021. https://blog.buddhagroove.com /the-history-purpose-and-value-of-meditation-mala-beads/.

Holleb, Morgan Lev Edward. *The A-Z of Gender and Sexuality: From Ace to Ze.* London: Jessica Kingsley Publishers, 2019.

Iantaffi, Alex, and Meg-John Barker. *How to Understand Your Gender: A Practical Guide for Exploring Who You Are.* London: Jessica Kingsley Publishers, 2018.

"Intersex." United Nations Human Rights, Office of the High Commissioner. Accessed October 13, 2020. https://www.unfe.org/wp-content /uploads/2018/10/Intersex-English.pdf.

Kliegman, Isabel Radow. *Tarot and the Tree of Life: Finding Everyday Wisdom in the Minor Arcana.* Wheaton, IL: Quest Books, 1997.

Knight, Gareth. *A Practical Guide to Qabalistic Symbolism.* Boston: Weiser, 2001.

L'Engle, Madeleine. *A Wrinkle in Time.* New York: Square Fish/Farrar, Straus and Giroux, 2012.

Matt, Daniel Chanan, trans. *Zohar: The Book of Enlightenment.* Mahwah, NJ: Paulist Press, 1983.

Magdalene, Misha. *Outside the Charmed Circle: Exploring Gender & Sexuality in Magical Practice.* Woodbury, MN: Llewellyn Publications, 2020.

Moler, Daniel. *Shamanic Qabalah: A Mystical Path to Uniting the Tree of Life & the Great Work*. Woodbury, MN: Llewellyn Publications, 2018.

Moore, Alan (writer), J. H. Williams III and Mick Gray (illustrators). *Promethea: Book 1*. New York: Vertigo/DC Comics, 2000.

———. *Promethea: Book 2*. New York: Vertigo/DC Comics, 2001.

———. *Promethea: Book 3*. New York: Vertigo/DC Comics, 2004.

———. *Promethea: Book 4*. New York: Vertigo/DC Comics, 2005.

———. *Promethea: Book 5*. New York: Vertigo/DC Comics, 2006.

Moore, Shameik, Jake Johnson, and Hailee Steinfeld. *Spider-Man: Into the Spider-Verse*. Directed by Bob Persichetti, Peter Ramsey, Rodney Rothman. Sony Pictures: 2018.

North, Ryan, and Erica Henderson. *The Unbeatable Squirrel Girl, Issue 19*. In *The Unbeatable Squirrel Girl Vol. 6: Who Run the World? Squirrels, Issues 17–22*. New York: Marvel Comics, 2017.

Penczak, Christopher. *The Temple of High Witchcraft: Ceremonies, Spheres, and the Witches' Qabalah*. Woodbury, MN: Llewellyn Publications, 2017.

Pollack, Rachel. *The Kabbalah Tree: A Journey of Balance & Growth*. St. Paul, MN: Llewellyn Publications, 2004.

Reed, Ellen Cannon. *The Witches Qabala: The Pagan Path and the Tree of Life*. Boston: Weiser Books, 1997.

Regardie, Israel. *A Garden of Pomegranates: An Outline of the Qabalah*. Los Angeles: New Falcon, 2019.

River, Lindsay, and Sally Gillespie. *The Knot of Time: Astrology and the Female Experience*. New York: Harper & Row, 1987.

Schnelbach, Leah. "8 Lessons MST3K Taught Me About Writing, Life, and Everything." June 26, 2013. https://www.tor.com/2013/06/26/life-lessons-from-mystery-science-theater-3000/.

Shulman, Jason. *Kabbalistic Healing: A Path to an Awakened Soul.* Rochester, VT: Inner Traditions, 2004.

Snow, Cassandra. *Queering the Tarot.* Newburyport, MA: Weiser, 2019.

———. *Queering Your Craft: Witchcraft from the Margins.* Newburyport, MA: Weiser, 2020.

Villarreal, Daniel. "What Does Queer Mean? Well, There's No One Definition." LGBTQ Nation. September 21, 2019. https://www.lgbtq nation.com/2019/09/queer-mean-well-theres-no-one-definition/.

Wang, Robert. *The Qabalistic Tarot: A Textbook of Mystical Philosophy.* York Beach, ME: Weiser Books, 1983.

Westcott, W. Wynn, trans. *Sepher Yetzirah.* Brampton, Ontario: Ballantrae Reprint, 1991.

"What Is Intersex?" Planned Parenthood. Accessed January 26, 2021. https://www.plannedparenthood.org/learn/gender-identity/sex-gender -identity/whats-intersex.

"WoLF Media Style Guide." Accessed December 29, 2020. https://www .womensliberationfront.org/news/wolf-media-style-guide.

Wright, Thomas J., dir. *Angel.* Season 2, episode 16. "Epiphany." Aired February 27, 2001, on WB Network.

Notes